T0056933

THE **INFRARED GRILL** MASTER

RECIPES AND TECHNIQUES FOR PERFECTLY SEARED, DELICIOUSLY SMOKY BBQ EVERY TIME

JENNY DORSEY

Published in the United States by:
ULYSSES PRESS
P.O. Box 3440
Berkeley, CA 94703
www.ulyssespress.com

ISBN: 978-1-64604-040-7
Library of Congress Control Number: 2020931850

Printed in the United States by Versa Press
10 9 8 7 6 5 4 3 2 1

Acquisitions editor: Casie Vogel
Managing editor: Claire Chun
Editor: Renee Rutledge
Proofreader: Kathy Kaiser
Front cover design: Beau Sims
Interior design and layout: what!design @ whatweb.com
Cover photographs: © Jenny Dorsey

NOTE TO READERS: This book has been written and published strictly for informational and educational purposes only. It is not intended to serve as medical advice or to be any form of medical treatment. You should always consult your physician before altering or changing any aspect of your medical treatment and/or undertaking a diet regimen, including the guidelines as described in this book. You should always consult your physician if concerned about potential allergies or consuming carcinogenic ingredients. Do not stop or change any prescription medications without the guidance and advice of your physician. Any use of the information in this book is made on the reader's good judgment after consulting with his or her physician and is the reader's sole responsibility. This book is not intended to diagnose or treat any medical condition and is not a substitute for a physician. Take special note of the important safety warnings throughout this book, and always use customary precautions for safe food preparation, handling, and storage.

This book is independently authored and published and no sponsorship or endorsement of this book by, and no affiliation with, any trademarked brands or other products mentioned within is claimed or suggested. All trademarks that appear in ingredient lists and elsewhere in this book belong to their respective owners and are used here for informational purposes only. The author and publisher encourage readers to patronize the quality brands mentioned and pictured in this book.

CONTENTS

CHAPTER 1

INTRODUCTION TO INFRARED TECHNOLOGY

WHAT IS INFRARED TECHNOLOGY?

After seeing infomercial after infomercial about infrared heaters, saunas, and grills, you are most likely wondering what infrared technology is. In short, it is the harnessing of **infrared radiation** (IR)—also referred to as **infrared light**—which is a type of electromagnetic radiation (or energy-carrying waves, which the common household microwave also emits) that is generally not visible to the human eye. It's a type of energy source that's commonly found in nature. For example, more than half the Sun's energy arrives on Earth in the form of IR that we never see, but is still absorbed by objects we then perceive to be a certain temperature (for example, the hot sand on the beach on a sunny day).

Given its nature, the use of IR is prolific across many industries. All objects above the temperature of absolute zero, generally considered the lowest temperature possible on Earth, emit infrared radiation, and measuring these radiation amounts via **thermal imaging** is widely applicable for everything from military surveillance to weather satellites to medical imaging. Since infrared light is invisible to the human eye, IR can be used to increase the amount of light for night vision without shining visible, bright light to illuminate the subject. And because IR can heat molecules quickly and directly (molecules absorb the energy-carrying waves and heat up), it's often utilized for both consumer and commercial projects where an efficient heat source is needed.

HOW DOES INFRARED GRILLING WORK?

"Infrared" has very much become a trendy term in the grilling world, touted as a way to heat up grills faster and more evenly, and for serving up juicier results than its gas or charcoal counterparts. The rapid mainstream ascent of infrared grilling is likely due to its patent (originally owned by Thermal Engineering Corporation, which still makes high-end infrared grills to this day) expiring in 2000, when other grill manufacturers were able to adapt the technology to their own devices. Although it's become a common selling point, many consumers are still unsure what advantages IR actually offers to their grilling routine or how best to take advantage of them. The easiest way to truly explain the power (and limitations) of infrared technology in your grill is to first delineate the various types of heat transfer in different styles of cooking, then break down the differences and similarities between the most common types of grills available: charcoal, gas, and infrared.

HEAT TRANSFER TYPES

There are three main types of heat transfer in cooking: conduction, convection, and radiation. **Conduction** cooks food via direct contact with a heating element, for example, sautéing some garlic in a skillet over the stove. In this case, the skillet is the heating element (which is also being heated directly by the electric or gas stove). The oil used in this instance is not considered the main heating mechanism to cook the food (unlike in convection, see below) but instead is a supporting material to the skillet to help the food cook more evenly and perhaps add flavor.

Convection cooking uses a secondary medium, such as gas or liquid, to cook food. For example, deep frying submerges food in large quantities of hot oil and boiling submerges it in water. The same mechanism goes for steaming, smoking, baking, and roasting food using hot air. Within this category, it's important to note that liquid convection is more powerful than gas convection and the denser the fluid being used, the faster the food will heat up. This is because the heat capacity of each medium is different. In other words, the temperature of something is not the same as the heat it can emit. This can most concisely be explained by the sheer fact that we can reach into a 350°F oven to pull out a finished cake but definitely cannot sink our hands into boiling water (212°F) to grab a potato.

Finally, **radiation** cooks food through direct contact with the heat source, like fire or gas or energy waves, not a hot heating element like a pan or grill grate. Broiling is the easiest to visualize here, where a food item is being cooked—often very aggressively—by a heat source above it. Cooking food in a spit over a campfire is also a good example. You're likely thinking at this point, What about grilling? Well, this is where each type of grill differs, and things become a little more complicated.

Let's start with the biggest visual indicator of a food item having been grilled: the crisp grill marks on the surface of the food. In this case, the food was directly touching the hot grill grates and has been cooked in part as a result of conduction, regardless of the heat source (e.g., gas, charcoal). You can definitely achieve this nice crosshatched exterior with any grill on the market. But the rest of grilling's essence? Let's dive into that below.

OUTDOOR GRILL TYPES

This book specifically talks about outdoor grills, which usually have some sort of contraption to cover the grill during cooking. This cover can be made of different materials, such as metal or ceramic, with some being more efficient at holding in the hot air than others. In all instances covering your grill during the cooking period creates convection heat by trapping the heat emitted by the heat source and warming up the air within the grill itself. The material of the cover also absorbs the heat but reemits some of it.

Now that we've established that all grills utilize both conduction and convection cooking, let's explore how radiation comes into play. What's confusing here is that the level of radiation in the cooking process depends on how the heat source is structured within the grill. The easiest way to think about that is to ask, What's in between the food and the heat source?

CHARCOAL GRILLS

Charcoal grills, which are almost always set up with hot, burning charcoal directly below a grill grate, are the most straightforward. The hot charcoal emits radiant heat, which cooks the food alongside conduction heat (the grill grates) and convection heat (the hot air with the grill covered). The major pros of charcoal grills are producing a smoky taste when fat drippings of the food hit the charcoal below and create smoke and flame, and the high radiant heat the coals achieve. The biggest con to charcoal grilling is the maintenance—both during the grilling session (swapping out spent coals, waiting for new coals to heat up) and afterward (cleaning up ashes and leftover coals), as well as the safety issues that come with having hot coals out in the open. It's also prone to flare-ups as there is no barrier between the heat source and the fat coming from the food.

GAS GRILLS

Gas grills, on the other hand, vary quite widely in terms of how they are built. Some emit direct flame below the grill grates, which is very similar to charcoal grills. (However, it's important to note charcoal burns hotter than gas.) Others heat secondary objects (e.g., lava rocks, ceramic briquettes, drip covers), which then emit radiant heat up to the food and, along with the conduction and convection heat, cook it.

While radiant heat is involved in these styles of gas grills and gas burns at 3,500°F, gas creates far less radiant heat than charcoal, so convection heat plays a much larger role here. The pros of gas grills can be distilled to ease of use and flexibility: unlike charcoal, you can control the level of flame in the grill, and there are thousands of different gas grills with accessories like a wood chip box to add smoke flavor to the food or a "searing station" that concentrates extra heat to be used for steaks and the like.

Speaking of the searing station, enter infrared radiation, which many gas grills employ *as* the searing station. You can consider this an infrared grill within a gas grill, though, in general, infrared grills are already a subset of gas grills (note that some can be electric as well).

INFRARED GRILLS

On infrared grills (or sear stations), the first heat source (e.g., gas or electricity) emits radiant heat to some style of infrared plate (usually ceramic, metal, or glass) or infrared rod (usually metal). This plate or rod is specially developed to have extremely high **thermal conductivity**, or the ability to absorb energy from the initial heat source, magnify it, and reemit it as invisible infrared waves, a powerful source of radiant heat, to cook the food while the grill grates and cover continue to contribute conductive and convective heat. Why do this triple-heating? That brings us to the next section.

WHY SHOULD I GRILL WITH INFRARED RADIATION?

There are two major benefits to grilling using infrared radiation versus the standard charcoal or gas grill. The first is the **directness of heat source**. Since infrared burners use special ceramic, metal, or glass to minimize the output of convection heat, the grill concentrates only radiation heat to reach the food. Infrared grill companies say this avoids the drying out of food common to grilling with convective heat (consider how, say, deep frying a chicken will dehydrate and crisp up the outside of the chicken while also cooking the interior). Some companies claim food retains up to 35% more of its juice, but it is difficult to objectively test this metric. However, infrared heat *is* more direct—its energy waves can move in all directions and it is not affected by air turbulence (such as outside wind with an open grill or the varying patterns of hot air inside a closed grill) until it reaches a solid object. In short, infrared radiation ensures food is heated via radiation and not convection, and thus provides far more even, consistent heat across the entire grill.

The second and arguably more publicized benefit of infrared grilling is **efficiency/temperature of the heat source**. Unlike much less powerful sources of radiant heat generated from a gas or electric source, the technology behind infrared ceramic, glass, and metal plates and rods creates far more concentrated energy waves at far higher temperatures (some grills boast up to 1,000°F). For meats meant to be some version of rare at the center, infrared grills cook extremely quickly due to their intense and efficient heat, minimizing the amount of time the food spends on the grill and ensuring a very lightly cooked center. This also helps keep infrared grills mostly smokeless, because stray fats and liquid from the food do not fall directly onto the heat source. This makes for an easier cleanup. A related fact is that infrared grills also preheat much faster than other options.

(Note: A higher temperature on an infrared grill does not mean it sears "better" but rather that it gets above 280°F, the temperature typically required for the **Maillard reaction**—where the browning and caramelization of protein sugars happen—faster than with other grills. It then holds that radiant heat longer to cook the whole food item faster.)

IS COOKING WITH INFRARED RADIATION SAFE?

According to current research on infrared radiation, it is not powerful enough to alter the molecular structure of food cooked using it as a heat source, and the resulting food is safe for human use and consumption. So far, no links have been found between infrared grilling and cancer, but it's important to note that links have been found between food cooked at high temperatures (especially for a long time) and carcinogenic compounds within the meat, which affects all types of grilling and high-heat cookery.

According to the National Cancer Institute, meats cooked at high temperatures above 300°F or those cooked for a long time (especially at high temperatures for a long time) tend to form more **heterocyclic amines** (HCAs), while food exposed to smoke during cooking produces **polycyclic aromatic hydrocarbons** (PAHs). Both of these compounds have been found to sometimes cause cancer in animals during lab experiments. The World Cancer Research Fund and the American Institute for Cancer Research recommend limiting consumption of processed meats but offer no specific guidelines on how much HCA and PAH to avoid. This is all to say, moderation when it comes to eating grilled food is key.

If you're comfortable with the above and still interested in infrared grilling, rest assured it is also comparatively safer than grills with an open flame. With charcoal or wood grills, the charcoal or wood itself leaves polluting particles (in addition to higher levels of PAHs) that can adversely affect your lungs. Additionally, the fat drippings that fall onto the flame and smoke also develop carcinogenic chemicals that are then transferred to the food. On an infrared grill, you'll still need to watch out for the consequences of high heat but, theoretically, less of these harmful compounds should form, and the actual cooking is safer too, with fewer flare-ups and less smoke.

CHAPTER 2

GETTING STARTED WITH INFRARED GRILLING

WHICH INFRARED GRILL IS RIGHT FOR YOU?

Hundreds of infrared grills from different manufacturers are available on the market today. There's no one right choice, so I find the following set of questions useful as a means to evaluate all the options.

WHAT WILL YOU BE COOKING ON YOUR INFRARED GRILL?

As explained in Chapter 1, grilling via infrared radiation has its pros and cons (as with all types of grills), so consider what will make up the bulk of your outdoor cooking. Will it be steaks and other meats meant to be seared quickly and served medium rare? Infrared is an excellent option in that case, as it can bring up surface temperatures very high and cook through meat very quickly. Choose a model that has a good, and very hot, searing surface.

Will it be ribs and brisket, or similar cuts meant for a long and slow cook? You can certainly still use infrared for that, but you'll need to look for grills that offer methods of amplifying convective heat (see page 6 in Chapter 1), such as raised racks or an indirect grilling side. You'll also need wider temperature controls from high to low as infrared is generally not fantastic at very low temperatures, so perhaps you could even consider a dual grill that has an infrared side and a separate gas section.

Will it be vegetables that you want smoke-kissed but crispy? Infrared is also excellent for that, and you'll need no special bells or whistles. Once you've determined the major groups of food you'll be cooking, you can decide if you want a grill that's purely infrared or contains another type of heat source, plus what types of accessories and structure are ideal.

WILL YOU BE SMOKING MEAT?

If you love the smell and taste of food made from charcoal or wood-based grills, ask yourself how much you want to deliver a similar final result. If you would consider this "nice to have," you can opt for a regular infrared grill and simply use wood chips when grilling (explained in more detail later on page 14) or opt for a fancier infrared grill that has a compartment for wood chips. If this is something you cannot part with (and you're comfortable with the cleanup required of charcoal and wood grills), opt for something that uses either or both charcoal and wood as well as infrared technology to cook so you can reap the benefits of infrared radiation (i.e., more even heat distribution) while seizing the smoky notes from those ingredients.

HOW OFTEN WILL YOU GRILL, FOR WHOM, AND WHERE?

If you grill very often and have a large outdoor area where there's space to set up a more advanced, heavy-duty grill, by all means select a higher-end infrared model and live your best life! If you most often grill on the go (such as while camping or during picnics), perhaps a more portable option would be better. There are some infrared grills that you can pack up like a suitcase! If you live in an apartment building and are grilling on your patio, perhaps you have regulations on outdoor appliances and it would be safest and easiest to opt for an electric infrared grill instead of a propane-fueled one. (You can also try an indoor infrared grill, but this book focuses on outdoor models.)

If the most common grilling scenario you find yourself in is for groups, you may want to prioritize a grill with more surface area so you can cook greater quantities at once. A grill with a warming zone may be a bonus here too, if you need to keep food hot between batches. If you usually cook for yourself or a small family, a smaller circular grill works well, and if you tend to have the occasional busy night of grilling look for one that allows for multiple rows of food.

WHAT TYPE OF GRILLER ARE YOU?

There is a learning curve associated with infrared grilling. If you're a hobbyist, you may want to select a smaller, less expensive grill to see if you like this style of grilling. If you're an advanced griller, you'll want to think through the abilities of each infrared grill to see if it meets your standards and can perform the different functions you're interested in using it for. Regardless of familiarity, a trial period is always a great idea if you're new to infrared and want to properly gauge how it may differ from the grilling you've done previously.

WHAT'S YOUR PRICE POINT?

There's an infrared grill for everyone out there, but, naturally, certain improvements will show on the bill. If you're not sure you want to commit hundreds of dollars to infrared yet, perhaps start with a basic electric one (under $200) to see how you feel about it. Propane versions can typically reach higher temperatures than their electric counterparts, so if you have the ability to use propane in your grilling area, it could be worth the extra cost for heat efficiency. If you have the budget, a dual-system infrared grill with gas or charcoal offers a great deal of additional flexibility. And finally, if this grill is your pièce de résistance, then why not nab the grill with the searing station, the indirect station, the vegetable station, the wood chips attachment, and the charcoal option?

ESSENTIAL TOOLS FOR GRILLING

Now that you're ready to get started with your infrared grill, make sure you have the essential tools for a successful session. Here's an essentials list for those starting out on grilling in general; frequent grillers new to infrared do not need any specific new tools.

Grill Brush: This is the first thing you absolutely will need, unless you have a grill with a ceramic or glass plate. A grill brush is a coarsely bristled brush that cleans the grates of your grill in between cooks. It's imperative you keep your grill clean (more on that in Infrared Grilling Best Practices and Safety on page 14) to prevent flare-ups and fires, plus clean grates ensure your food doesn't stick to the grill and flavors don't blend together in your food. Choose a brush with heat-resistant hairs (like stainless steel) as the best time to clean your grill is when it's warm (during a preheat) and any lodged food particles are pliable enough for removal.

Long Tongs: The bigger your grill, the more useful longer tongs are so less of your body is exposed to the heat from the grill. While infrared grilling has no direct flames or smoldering charcoal, it will certainly still feel hot over the panel of radiation. Especially if you have many items being grilled at once, investing in some long tongs is an ideal way to minimize heat exposure to your arms.

Fish Spatula: This spatula is made for flipping fish but can be used for flipping anything on the grill that should be handled delicately (like homemade burgers, for example). Make sure you buy one made of stainless steel that is thin enough to slide easily between the food and the grate.

Internal Temperature Thermometer: Food safety is paramount to cooking, so a temperature probe is hugely helpful to ensure all food (especially meat, seafood, and poultry) is cooked to the proper internal temperature. Make sure to wash the probe thoroughly after using and keep it in a clean location—the last thing you want is to be injecting bacteria into future meats with a dirty thermometer!

Small Brush: Many items going on the grill need a light sheen of oil to keep them from sticking to the grate. This convenient little tool distributes oil evenly to all types of foods, from chicken breast to asparagus. Plus, you'll end up using less oil this way!

Metal Skewers: Forget the hassle of soaking wooden skewers. Choose some hardy metal skewers that you can wash and reuse forever. Plus, you can use these skewers over high heat without worrying they may burn.

Resting Rack: This is a must-have for all types of protein cookery as it allows for even air circulation all around your finished piece of meat, poultry, or fish to minimize carryover cooking (explained in more detail on page 16). I like having a few resting racks (quarter sheet, half sheet, full sheet) so I can pick an appropriate size for what I'm grilling and not take up unnecessary space. That being said, you can rest vegetables and other items on the rack as well!

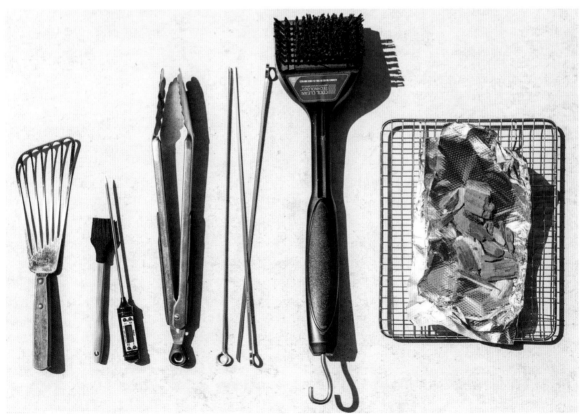

Wood Chips: Yes, you can infuse some smoky backbone to your foods without a special smoker, even with an entry-level infrared grill! Some of my favorite options are mesquite (for that classic BBQ scent) and pecan (for more delicate cuts). Alder is also excellent and tastes particularly good with vegetables.

Note: There's a lot of discourse on whether wood chips/chunks should be soaked prior to being used on the grill. Traditionally, wood chips/chunks are soaked not necessarily to slow their burn rate (as wood absorbs very little water, even after long periods of soaking, and will burn in roughly the same amount of time) but rather to dampen the intensity of classic charcoal grills and create steam in the grill. It's technically not necessary (I don't bother), but how you'd like to approach it is up to you. If you do want to soak your wood, make sure to add it to the grill, then give the grill about 5 minutes to rise back up in temperature as the water dripping onto the infrared plate or coil will lower the temperature.

INFRARED GRILLING BEST PRACTICES AND SAFETY

Cooking on an infrared grill does take a little practice and getting used to, especially if you're accustomed to working with gas or charcoal grills. Below are some guidelines to combat the initial frustration with any learning curve and help you feel more comfortable with your new infrared grill faster.

CHECK YOUR FOOD OFTEN

Infrared grills can reach extremely high surface temperatures, and their cooking heat is more direct than that of other grill types. As a result, food may cook faster than what you're used to, so a good rule of thumb is to check your item halfway into your "regular" cooking time to assess its level of doneness in comparison to your other grill until you become acclimated to the timing of your infrared.

The good news is that infrared radiation delivers a much more consistent heat source than most other styles of grills, so once you've gotten into a rhythm and assessed the general timetable for cooking your most common food items, your grill will continue to deliver consistent results over its entire surface without hot or cold spots.

CHECK SURFACE TEMPERATURES AND USE AN INTERNAL THERMOMETER

Due to its location, often on the lid of the grill, the built-in thermometer gauge is often not a completely accurate reflection of the actual temperature within the grill. Not only that, the general air temperature of the grill is very different from the surface temperature of the grates, and an infrared grill can heat to much higher temperatures than its counterparts. It's best to use an infrared temperature gun to check grate temperatures and compare that to the built-in thermometer so you can sense what the typical difference is between the two. Using a meat thermometer to check for doneness the first few times you cook with infrared is also a good way to adjust for different cooking times and doneness markers on the new grill.

TRIM THE FAT

Infrared grills cook with radiation instead of convection, as explained in Chapter 1. This results in less hot air circulating in the grill itself, compared to gas or charcoal. While the verdict is still out on whether this makes the final food products more juicy, it does visibly affect the look of the exterior. Namely, ultra-fatty cuts don't dehydrate on the surface the way they do on other grills. For example, achieving a crispy bacon or the nice crunch of dark meat chicken skin is somewhat challenging in the infrared because these fatty surfaces are not drying and shrinking as much throughout the cooking process (due to less hot air in the grill). Additionally, infrareds tend to cook food faster so there's less time to render said fat. This isn't to say you can't cook fattier cuts on an infrared grill, but rather that it's particularly great for lean cuts, and that a little fat goes a long way. (Note: This is why infrareds are favored for steaks, as with steaks you want to preserve the inner marbling by quickly instigating the Maillard reaction on the surface of the meat for that caramelized look and taste.)

CLEAN YOUR GRILL!

The importance of keeping your grill clean cannot be overstated. Infrared grills are multi-layered appliances with many nooks and crannies that need to be kept free of debris like excess fat, burned wood chips, and food particles. Not only do these blockages impede your infrared grill's direct heat efficacy by adding additional objects between the heat and your food, they also constitute a fire hazard. Especially in models where the heating mechanism is exposed to the food (for example, in the electric infrared grill, the infrared coil sits directly below the grates), a pileup of spent wood and caked-on grease can easily ignite. This destroys your food, creates carcinogenic smoke that enters your food and lungs, and is dangerous for everyone around you. *If a fire does occur, put it out using salt (It's a good idea to keep a 3-pound box in the house). NEVER use water on a grease fire as oil and water do not mix, and it will expand the fire.*

Make sure to review your manufacturer's instructions for how best to clean your infrared grill. While you may not need to do an in-depth clean *every* time you grill, putting some time in for short cleans after each cooking session and scheduling a regular deep clean is a good way to keep your infrared grill happy for a long time to come.

GENERAL GRILLING TERMS AND GUIDELINES

For those new to grilling, the infrared part is only the first step in the equation. Grilling is a whole new niche within the culinary sphere, with devotees around the world who write about tricks, tips, and the science behind the process. This is an endless, wonderful journey to go on, so here are some initial topics, terms, and guidelines to whet your palate.

CARRYOVER COOKING

Removing food from the grill (or any other heat source) does not immediately stop the cooking cycle; instead, the internal temperature of the food will continue to climb even as the exterior begins to cool. The effect of this **carryover cooking** is that foods you're attempting to cook to a specific temperature—say, a steak to medium rare at 135°F—will actually be overcooked by the time it's been taken off the heat and allowed to rest or sit undisturbed (preferably over a resting rack, as mentioned on page 13) for a few minutes.

Mastering your timing to remove food from the grill in anticipation of carryover cooking is a blend of art and science, as all foods are different shapes and sizes. A general rule of thumb is to anticipate a 5 to 10°F increase in the internal temperature of your food after a proper rest. The larger the food item, the greater this rise in temperature tends to be and the longer you'll need to wait during the resting period. The heat level the food is cooked at also matters, as more heat will be absorbed by the food in hotter conditions and result in greater carryover (and more time needed for resting).

For this reason, all recipes in this book will guide you to remove your meat from the grill when it is 5 to 10°F *below* the target internal temperature of that item.

RESTING

If you'll be grilling meat on your infrared, make sure to budget time to properly rest your meat after it's been removed from the grill. Not only does this allow carryover cooking to run its due course, it is crucial to retaining the flavorful juices within the meat. When meat cooks, especially at a high temperature, it rapidly releases moisture from within the muscle fibers to the surface, which we witness in the form of a satisfying sizzle. (It's also interesting to note the amount of liquid released increases past 140°F, which is why medium rare at 130 to 135°F is so popular.) Once meat has been cooked to the desired doneness level, letting the finished product rest gives its moisture a chance to redistribute within the meat so when you slice into it, that juiciness stays in the food and doesn't pool onto your plate.

If you're unsure when to cut into your meat after cooking, use your internal temperature probe and check for when your cut reaches 120 to 125°F. If you prefer your food warmer, you can of course cut into it faster (after a shorter resting period) but the tradeoff is more moisture loss. If you're particularly gung ho for a perfect steak with the least amount of gray area (the overcooked meat on the way to achieving the medium rare in the middle of the steak), try your hand at the **reverse sear method,** where meat is cooked to the proper temperature at a low temperature via convection (sous vide is especially popular for this) then seared very quickly at extremely high temperatures for an even crust.

The ideal way to rest cooked meat is to place it on a resting rack set on a sheet tray in a cool place, as this allows for cool air flow all around the meat.

SMOKING

Smoking is another subset within the grilling community, and enthusiasts can discuss endlessly the "best" variation of smoking any food item. In short, **smoking** food entails cooking it using the smoke of some material, usually woods such as oak, hickory, or apple. For those with a dedicated smoker, food can be **hot smoked** at temperatures between 126 and 176°F, or **cold smoked** at temperatures in the range of 68 to 86°F (though cold smoking does not fully cook foods). In the case of infrared grills, the kinds that offer a smoking option often utilize an accessory, like a wood tray, to capture the smoke from the wood and mingle it with the food while the main cooking method is the heat of the grill, not the hot smoke. This is most commonly referred to as "barbecuing" or "pit roasting."

If you're new to smoking using a grill, experiment with wood chips or chunks you know you like (or a relatively neutral one like oak) by placing them in the wood tray *or* directly on the grates, covering the grill, and letting them begin to smoke. Then, proceed with cooking your food, taking care to cover the grill as much as possible to capture the smoke. Naturally, you'll find smokier characteristics in foods that require more time on the grill and have longer access to the smoke, though if you love a super-smoky taste, heftier woods like mesquite or hickory can help you get to the desired level of smokiness faster.

OIL YOUR FOOD, NOT YOUR GRATES

There are mixed messages on what exactly to oil before a grilling session to prevent meat, fish, and vegetables from sticking to grill grates. Contrary to much literature out there, oiling the *food* that's meant to be cooked and placing it on a hot, clean grill delivers far more consistent results than putting unoiled food on a hot, clean, oiled grill. I know this anecdotally from working at many restaurants with gas and wood-burning grills; but scientifically speaking, oiling the meat with oil that has a high smoke point (such as grapeseed, with a smoke point of 450°F) allows the oil to smooth out the minuscule abrasions on the grill grates while the water emitted by the food helps separate the food from the grate. Plus, this avoids any off flavors that are caused by oil being heated above its smoke point, which is more common when the grates themselves are oiled.

EVALUATE YOUR MEAT ON THICKNESS, NOT WEIGHT

Grilling timetables vary widely due to the exact shape and size of what is being grilled, which is why all the times in this book give both ranges *and* another metric to inspect doneness. As you're working through the first few chickens, steaks, and other food items, try to start taking some visual inventory of how thick they are in relation to how long it takes for each item to cook. Thickness is much more helpful to maintaining consistency than weight: You can cook several 1-pound rib eye steaks and see them finish at different times due to different thicknesses, or the amount of solid matter the infrared grill must penetrate to cook the food in question. It's best to keep batches of items of similar thicknesses cooking at once so one does not overcook while another is still undercooked.

NOT ALL GRILLING IS ABOUT DIRECT HEAT, HOT TEMPERATURE

Getting a handle on indirect grilling and maximizing indirect heat sources of your infrared grill will truly take your grilling game to the next level. Many grills will come with additional racks (such as a warming rack or warming station) that is perfect for adding a lovely smoke to your food while continuing to cook it very gently—perfect for tougher cuts with lots of connective tissue that benefit from long cook times and low heat, like lamb shanks or prime rib.

You can also use the indirect grilling method for more tender cuts like sirloin steak if you have a particularly thick piece. Similar to searing a steak and finishing it in the oven, giving a quick sear on high heat combined with a cooler, longer finish ensures the outsides don't burn on the way to medium rare. Delicate items like whole fish benefit from softer treatment this way too. Char its skin, then let it finish its cook gradually over indirect heat. Juicy vegetables like enoki mushrooms and zucchini also stay succulent when wrapped in aluminum foil and cooked this way, absorbing flavor without removing moisture.

LEARN WHEN TO OPEN OR CLOSE YOUR GRILL

While one of the selling points of infrared grills is cooking with radiant heat versus convective heat, sometimes you need (or want) a little bit of both. This is where opening or closing your grill lid comes in. When the grill lid is closed, you trap the hot air within the grill, which could be a source of flavor (if you're also using this as a way to smoke your food) or slight moisture (from the steam that's escaping from the food and hitting the hot surface of the grates and/or heat source). This hot air also adds convective heat to the cooking equation, helping cook through larger items or higher volumes of items faster on the grill. Think of this as akin to placing your food in a hot oven.

On the other hand, if you want a quick kiss of conductive heat alongside the infrared grill's radiation, you can leave the grill lid open so the food doesn't cook through too much. This is ideal for high-temperature searing of food that's meant to be rare or raw at the center (e.g., filet mignon, scallops) or giving a light char to delicate items like vegetables meant to be left crunchy (e.g., pickles, radishes).

It's also worth mentioning that even though infrared grills don't produce as *much* smoke as a gas or charcoal grill, in closed-lid instances it still produces *some* smoke. When opening the lid of your grill, always be careful, open slowly, and stand at roughly a foot's distance to start.

CHAPTER 3

TROUBLESHOOTING YOUR INFRARED GRILL

MY MEAT IS OVERCOOKED

Your infrared grill is likely cooking the meat at either a hotter temperature or with a more direct heat (or both) than you're used to. Check your meat about halfway into its regular cooking cycle to see how its doneness compares to a former cooking style, and use a temperature gun to confirm what temperature the grilling surface/grates are before you start.

MY MEAT IS BURNED ON THE OUTSIDE, BUT STILL RAW ON THE INSIDE

The temperature on the grates of an infrared grill can go much higher than the temperature control states. Use a temperature gun to confirm what temperature the grilling surface/grates are before you start, and use exceedingly high temperatures only for searing or charring food items. Once seared or charred, lower the temperature of the grill to 350 to 400°F to continue cooking more evenly inside and out.

THE FAT ON MY MEAT IS CHEWY AND UNAPPETIZING. WHY?

Infrared grills cook with radiant heat versus convective, so there is generally less hot air circulating inside the grill. Because of this, exterior fat on meat does not react in the same way as it would in a gas or charcoal grill, where it often dehydrates, renders, and shrinks deliciously. This doesn't mean the fat isn't being cooked, but rather it's being heated more directly at a high temperature versus being slowly cooked down at a slightly lower one. (This is why fat-coated meats like duck breast are started in a cold pan and slowly warmed to coax out all the fat instead of seared in a hot pan.) It's best to trim fattier cuts before grilling, or perhaps consider rendering them on the stovetop before finishing on the grill.

THERE ISN'T ANY SMOKE FLAVOR ON MY FOOD EVEN THOUGH I USED WOOD CHIPS. WHY?

Your food likely wasn't in contact with the smoke long enough to absorb the flavors you wanted, or there weren't enough wood chips to create much smoke in the grill. Make sure to use high-quality wood chips (or wood chunks, which last longer but take a little more time to begin smoking) and let them really start smoking *before* placing your food onto the grill, especially if they are foods that cook quickly. You'll need to close your grill to ensure the smoke and food properly mix together, so if you're concerned about overcooking certain foods you can start the grill hot to start smoking the wood, lower the temperature, and grill your desired food. *Or,* place your food on a rack to remove it from direct contact with the grates, and let it cook through mostly convective heat.

WHY ISN'T MY GRILL GETTING HOT?

Infrared grills typically preheat faster than their counterparts, but they still need time to preheat. Keep the grill covered and preheat for a solid 8 to 10 minutes without disturbance.

WHY ISN'T MY GRILL STAYING HOT ONCE I OPEN THE LID?

Theoretically, the beauty of infrared grills is that they pack a punch with radiant heat instead of relying on conductive or convective heat. However, the reality is that entry-level models have trouble maintaining as high of a temperature as their more expensive, advanced counterparts. In my trials with an electric infrared grill, the temperature on the grill dropped 25°F or more every time I uncovered my grill. There isn't much you can do to "fix" this on your grill, but rather something to get used to and find workarounds for (unless you want to simply buy a better grill). The best workaround is to simply develop cooking timetables where you keep your grill's lid on during cooking *or* preheat your grill to the highest temperature it can go, get the conductive heat sear or char you desire, move your food to a rack where it can cook indirectly, and close the lid.

WHY IS THERE A HOT SPOT OR COLD SPOT ON MY GRILL?

Hot or cold spots are the result of the heat source being stronger/weaker in certain areas of the grill than others. While this shouldn't be as common in infrared grills as in other styles because the radiation isn't affected by things like proximity to the grill's opening, entry-level models especially may have some inconsistencies in the heat source being used to fire up the infrared plate or coil that can't realistically be fixed without upgrading to a nicer grill.

On the other hand, if the hot or cold spots are a sudden thing, perhaps there is some solid buildup on the grates or heat source of that area, which is blocking the infrared grill's waves.

MY FOOD KEEPS STICKING TO THE GRILL!

Make sure to bring your food (especially meat and fish) to room temperature before grilling so it doesn't emit as much steam, and oil it well. Clean your grill grates well (best to do so when the grill is hot so food can be removed easily), but do not oil the grates themselves. Preheat the grill and make sure the grates are hot (they should be 400°F or higher—check with a temperature gun!) before you place food on it. Finally, make sure you aren't trying to remove the food too soon after you place it on the grill grates. If you've followed the above directions, the food should be easy to remove once it's ready!

FOOD FROM MY GRILL HAS A STRANGE OFF-TASTE. WHY?

There are two common culprits for this. If you haven't cleaned your grill in a while, the residue of past wood and food scraps are likely burning and marring the taste of your food. Alternatively, if you are oiling your grates or oiling your food with oil that has a low smoke point (such as olive oil), that oil is surging past its smoke point on the grill, carbonizing, and leaving a bitter aftertaste. It's best to oil your food, *not* the grates, and do so with an oil that has a high smoke point, like grapeseed.

MY GRILL IS PRODUCING SO MUCH SMOKE!

This is likely because there's excess fat, wood chips, or debris that is intermittently catching on fire as you grill. Make sure to keep your grill well cleaned between uses and prevent buildup in both the drip tray and anywhere that touches the heat source. You may also have used too many wood chips or have too much oil or fat on what you're cooking. It's best to start with a handful of wood chips, trim excess fat off meats before grilling, and oil food items with a brush or misting spray instead of dipping or drizzling with oil.

CHAPTER 4

BEEF, PORK, AND GAME

FAUX AGED STEAK

Koji aged steak burst onto the scene in 2016 after a *Bon Appétit* article made the rounds proclaiming rubbing steak with the fungus koji (also known as *aspergillus oryzae*) and letting it sit for 48 hours will mimic the taste of a 28-day aged steak. (*Bon Appétit* credits the original idea to Chef Jonathon Sawyer of now-shuttered Trentina in Cleveland.) It makes a lot of sense: koji has long been used to break down the proteins of rice and soybeans to produce products such as miso, soy sauce, and sake.

For this faux aged steak, you can buy dried koji rice (readily available on Amazon and in Japanese grocery stores) and spread it all over a high-quality steak. Place the steak uncovered in the refrigerator to let the koji slowly begin to work its magic while the meat simultaneously sheds some moisture and compresses its flavor. The end result is a steak with a subtle sweetness and lovely depth that is meaty yet mellow at the same time. After you've mastered this technique, you can also begin to apply it to other cuts of meat and you'll see how endless the possibilities are with koji!

---

1 pound (1- to 1½-inch-thick) rib eye steak

⅓ cup koji rice, ground in a spice grinder to a fine powder

wood chips of choice, as needed (optional)

1½ teaspoons kosher salt

8 to 10 cracks freshly ground pepper

½ lemon

---

1. Dry the rib eye steak with paper towels and place it on a resting rack over a sheet tray.

2. Rub the koji rice powder to thoroughly cover the rib eye steak. Place the steak in the refrigerator, uncovered, and cure for 48 hours.

3. Remove the rib eye from the refrigerator and scrape off the koji rice crust with a spoon.

4. Bring the rib eye to room temperature, approximately 30 minutes. This will prevent the steak from emitting too much steam when it is being cooked (the result of a cold item being heated), as this would dampen the grill marks and potentially cause sticking to the grill.

5. While the rib eye is coming up to temperature, fire the grill on high until the temperature of the grill reaches 500°F. Add the wood chips, if using.

6. Salt the rib eye, then place it on the grill with the desired presentation side down. Grill, uncovered, for 3 to 5 minutes or until crisp grill marks appear. The first side that is grilled will always look slightly better than the other side as meat will naturally release its moisture under heat, thus making the second side a little too damp for a crisp, clean sear or grill mark.

7. Flip the rib eye. Insert an oven or grill-safe temperature thermometer set to the desired level of doneness into the thickest part of the rib eye. Cover the grill. Once the rib eye has reached the desired level of doneness (for medium rare, usually another 2 to 3 minutes), remove the rib eye from the grill and allow it to rest 5 minutes before slicing.

8. Finish the steak with ground pepper and a squeeze of lemon.

9. Slice the rib eye, if desired, and serve.

PRO TIP

For the best sear, leave the grill uncovered after you place the steak down for the first time. This ensures there's hot, direct heat on the surface of the steak, but no moisture that would dilute the crispness of the grill marks. It also helps ensure the steak does not cook through too quickly. Once you flip the steak, cover the grill to use convective heat to finish cooking through the entirety of the meat.

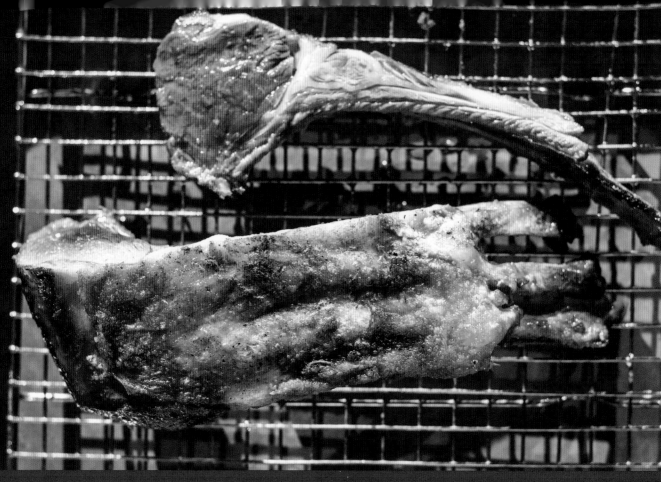

GRILLED LAMB CHOPS WITH RED PEPPER AND FENNEL RELISH

Contrary to popular belief, a high-quality spring lamb doesn't have such an overwhelming flavor that it must be paired with aggressive spices and accompaniments. I wanted to showcase how surprisingly sublime lamb can taste by using fresher, brighter ingredients that are often reserved for milder proteins like fish or chicken. This dish just might change your approach to lamb as a category!

YIELD: 4 servings | **PREP TIME:** 20 minutes | **COOK TIME:** 20 minutes

FOR THE GRILLED LAMB CHOPS

wood chips of choice, as needed (optional)

1 rack of lamb, frenched

kosher salt, to taste

neutral oil, to taste

FOR THE RED PEPPER AND FENNEL RELISH

2 red bell peppers, cored, quartered

1 bulb fennel, cored, quartered

½ cup finely chopped fresh parsley

¼ cup finely chopped fresh mint

6 cloves garlic, grated

4 scallions, minced

¼ cup extra-virgin olive oil

3 tablespoons sherry vinegar

2 teaspoons yondu

¼ teaspoon ground white pepper

kosher salt, to taste

white sugar, to taste

1. Preheat the grill to 450°F. Add the wood chips, if using.

2. Liberally salt the lamp chops on both sides, then brush them with oil. Set aside.

3. Place the red bell peppers and fennel, cut side down, on the grill. Cover and cook for 5 minutes, or until crisp grill marks appear.

4. Flip the red bell peppers and fennel. Cover and grill for another 2 to 3 minutes, or until cooked through. Remove from the grill and cool.

5. Once the red bell peppers are cool to the touch, carefully remove any charred skins, center seeds, and stems. Mince and reserve.

6. Once the fennel is cool to the touch, mince and reserve.

7. Combine the parsley, mint, garlic, scallions, red bell peppers, fennel, olive oil, sherry vinegar, yondu, and white pepper in a medium bowl. Add salt and sugar to taste. Place the relish in the refrigerator to marinate.

8. Place the rack of lamb on the grill, convex (outer) side down, and cook 5 to 8 minutes or until crisp grill marks appear.

9. Flip the rack of lamb over, cover, and cook another 3 to 5 minutes or to desired level of doneness.

10. Remove the rack of lamb from the grill and allow it to rest for 5 minutes.

11. Slice the rack of lamb into multiple chops and serve with the reserved relish.

YONDU

Yondu is an excellent vegetable-based seasoning that adds an interesting umami to dishes. It hails from South Korea and is widely available at Korean grocery stores. If you don't have yondu, you can substitute Maggi, fish sauce, or, if you must, Worcestershire sauce.

KIWI-MARINATED PORK TENDERLOIN

You may be surprised to learn that kiwis are a secret weapon for meat enthusiasts who want to tenderize tougher cuts quickly, naturally, and without any residual marinade flavor. Kiwis, alongside their tropical cousins papayas and pineapples, all contain the enzyme actinidin that helps break down the collagen structure of meat, resulting in a softer texture. However, be careful not to leave your meat in a kiwi mixture too long as it will begin to disintegrate and taste like mush. You don't need many kiwis to work this magic, and you can recycle "used" kiwis for a second batch of meats as well.

In this recipe, I used pork tenderloin, even though it's already a tender cut of pork, because I wanted to see how I could stretch kiwi's powers for delicate cuts and was pleasantly surprised at how delicious the end results were. Feel free to experiment with other cuts, like shoulder or butt, to experience kiwis' full range firsthand!

YIELD: 2–4 servings | **PREP TIME**: 10 minutes active, plus 1 hour to marinate | **COOK TIME**: 25 minutes

---

2 pork tenderloins (approximately 2 pounds)

kosher salt, as needed

2 kiwis, peeled and pureed

neutral oil, as needed

wood chips of choice, as needed (optional)

DIJON AND GREEN BELL PEPPER SAUCE

1 tablespoon neutral oil

1 tablespoon minced garlic

¼ cup minced shallots

2 green bell peppers, cored and minced

1 teaspoon fish sauce

2 sprigs thyme, leaves only

1 tablespoon Dijon mustard

½ lime, juiced

kosher salt, to taste

white sugar, to taste

---

1. Lightly salt the pork tenderloins, then combine with kiwi puree in large mixing bowl until covered.

2. Cover and let marinate for 1 hour in the refrigerator, then remove any excess marinade by scraping off by hand.

3. Preheat the grill to 450°F. Add the wood chips, if using.

4. In a medium skillet, heat the tablespoon of oil over medium heat until the skillet is slick and shiny.

5. Add the garlic, the shallots, and a dash of salt. Lower heat to medium-low and cook 2 to 3 minutes, or until the garlic is very fragrant and the shallots are translucent.

6. Add the green bell peppers, fish sauce, and thyme. Increase the heat to medium and cook 2 to 3 minutes, or until the peppers are softened but still bright green.

7. Turn heat off.

8. Stir in the Dijon mustard and lime juice, then season with salt and sugar to taste.

9. Sprinkle the marinated tenderloins with salt, then brush with additional oil, as needed.

10. Place the tenderloin on the grill. Cover and cook for 5 to 8 minutes, or until crisp grill marks appear.

11. Flip the tenderloin. Cover and cook for another 5 to 8 minutes, or until it reaches an internal temperature of 135°F.

12. Remove the tenderloin from the grill and allow it to rest for 5 minutes before slicing.

GRILLED BEEF TARTARE

Beef tartare is my must-order whenever I see it on a restaurant menu. I like to use boneless beef short rib (a cut of beef from the shoulder) as it has nice marbling for a buttery mouthfeel but is still toothsome for a substantive bite when eating. In this version, I grill the beef just a touch to bring char and texture to the final tartare. Instead of Worcestershire, I like to use yondu, a Korean seasoning brimming with salty umami that I find to be less aggressive and far more sublime. You can opt out of the mustard "caviar" if you're pressed for time, though I highly recommend making a batch because the little burst of vinegar against the bitterness of mustard is just as luxurious as the real stuff *and* can be used for far more applications.

YIELD: 3–4 servings | **PREP TIME:** 15 minutes | **COOK TIME:** 60 minutes

wood chips of choice, as needed (optional)	neutral oil, as needed
1 pound boneless beef short ribs	2 tablespoons thinly sliced chives
1 teaspoon kosher salt	2 cloves garlic, grated

1 teaspoon Dijon mustard

1 teaspoon green peppercorns in brine, drained, minced finely

1 dash white sugar

½ teaspoon toasted sesame oil

1 teaspoon yondu

½ teaspoon kosher salt

MUSTARD "CAVIAR"

¼ cup yellow mustard seeds

¼ cup apple cider vinegar

2 teaspoons kosher salt

1 teaspoon sherry vinegar

2 teaspoons extra-virgin olive oil

1 dash fennel pollen (optional)

1 large raw egg yolk per ¼ pound tartare, to serve (optional)

1 cup chicharróns per ¼ pound tartare, to serve (optional) (I like the Utz brand)

1 teaspoon white sugar

4 cups water

---

1. Preheat the grill to 500°F. Add the wood chips, if using.

2. Sprinkle the short ribs with salt on all sides, then brush with oil.

3. Place the short ribs on the grill and cook, uncovered, for 2 to 3 minutes on each side or until crisp black grill marks appear.

4. Remove the short ribs from the grill and place in the freezer, uncovered. Freeze 15 minutes or until the short ribs feel firm to the touch but are not frozen through.

5. Combine all of the ingredients for the mustard caviar in a pressure cooker.

6. Pressure cook on high for 30 minutes, then natural release and strain. Reserve.

7. Remove the short ribs from the freezer and slice against the grain into thin strips. Dice finely.

8. Combine the short ribs with the chives, garlic, mustard, peppercorns, sugar, sesame oil, yondu, salt, vinegar, olive oil, and fennel pollen, if using.

9. Dollop 1 large spoonful of mustard caviar on top.

10. Divide tartare into 4 servings (¼ pound each).

11. With ¼ pound tartare, place on serving plate, create a small well at the center of the tartare, and place a raw egg yolk on top, if using.

12. Serve with chicharróns, if using.

PRO TIP

If you don't have a pressure cooker, simply boil the mustard seeds in a small pot on the stovetop for 1 hour. Just make sure to double the liquid ingredients and the time, then cover the pot so it doesn't reduce too quickly.

FENNEL AND CORIANDER–RUBBED BABY BACK RIBS

I whip up these crowd-pleasing ribs anytime there's a BBQ among my circle of friends. They carry all the smoky meatiness guests are looking for in a riblet, but also an unexpected floral note and subtle sweetness that make them extremely easy to crave. One of my favorite experiments is to vary the type of wood chips I'm using while grilling this low and slow, as it adds a different complexity to the ribs every time. If it's your first time making ribs, make sure to keep an eye on these as they near the 1-hour finish line so you don't overcook them. The meat should be fork-tender, pulling away easily from the bone but not *falling* off (that's a misnomer!).

YIELD: 2–4 servings | PREP TIME: 5 minutes, plus 24 hours to marinate | COOK TIME: 1½ hours

1 rack (roughly 2 pounds) baby back ribs

FOR THE BRINE

2 quarts water

⅓ cup kosher salt

¼ cup light brown sugar

4 cloves garlic, sliced

1 shallot, sliced

FOR THE DRY RUB

1 teaspoon whole fennel seeds

2 teaspoons whole juniper berries

1 teaspoon whole black peppercorns

½ teaspoon whole cumin seeds

½ teaspoon whole nigella seeds

1 teaspoon whole coriander seeds

¼ teaspoon ground ancho chile

FOR GRILLING

1 tablespoon neutral oil

wood chips of choice, as needed

FOR BASTING

1 tablespoon maple syrup

½ cup apple cider vinegar

1 tablespoon soy sauce

---

1. Whisk the brine ingredients together in a large bowl until the salt and sugar fully dissolve. Place the ribs and brine in a suitably sized container or sealable bags. Brine for 24 hours in the refrigerator.

2. Remove the ribs from the brine and dry thoroughly with paper towels.

3. Preheat the grill to 450°F. Place wood chips of choice on grill.

4. Combine the dry rub ingredients in a spice grinder and coarsely grind. Rub over the ribs on a cutting board, concave side first. *This keeps the spices from sticking to the board after you flip the ribs.*

5. To grill, drizzle the oil on the convex side of the ribs, distributing evenly.

6. Place the ribs on the grill and cook, uncovered, for 15 minutes or until the surface is lightly charred and the spices have browned but are not burned.

7. Move the ribs to the upper grill rack, away from the direct heat of the grill.

8. Turn the grill temperature down to 350°F, cover, and cook for 1 hour, or until the meat is fork-tender and comes off easily from the bone.

9. Mix the maple syrup, apple cider vinegar, and soy sauce in a small bowl. Pour the mixture over the ribs 2 to 3 times during the hour-long cook.

10. Remove the ribs from the grill and allow them to rest 5 minutes before slicing into individual riblets.

BEEF STEW WITH LEEKS AND KIMCHI

Kimchi will transform anything you have at home into something better. No matter how sparse your pantry or refrigerator is, rest assured that kimchi can make that can of black beans, box of spaghetti, or half bag of lentils really shine. (It's also a great probiotic!) This recipe harmonizes kimchi's natural fermented umami with that of beef, pork, chicken, and Korean soybean paste, or doenjang, to take this humble stew to the next level. Some call doenjang "Korean miso"; however, it is actually very different as it does *not* use koji as a starter, fermenting the soybeans with salt only. For soups and stews, I like to use flavored varieties that contain anchovy, shrimp, or crab to add some of shellfish's natural umami to the mix too! (Doenjang is widely available in Korean grocery stores like H Mart, or online.)

YIELD: 2–4 servings | **PREP TIME:** 20 minutes | **COOK TIME:** 2 hours

1 pound beef stew meat

kosher salt, to taste

1 chorizo sausage, split lengthwise

2 leeks, white parts only, split lengthwise

3 Yukon gold potatoes or red potatoes, halved

1 tablespoon neutral oil, plus more for brushing

3 stalks celery, chopped

4 cloves garlic, grated

1 tablespoon Korean soybean paste

1 cup kimchi, sliced, with juices

2 quarts unsalted chicken stock

mesquite wood chips, as needed

white sugar, to taste

lemon juice, to taste

¼ cup chopped sweet basil

1. Preheat the grill to 450°F.

2. Sprinkle the beef stew meat with salt and brush lightly with oil.

3. Place the stew meat and the chorizo with its cut side down on the grill. Cover and cook for 5 minutes, or until crisp grill marks appear.

4. Flip the stew meat and chorizo. Cover and cook for another 3 to 5 minutes, or until crisp grill marks appear.

5. Remove the stew meat and chorizo from the grill. Set the stew meat aside. Cool the chorizo, then slice.

6. Place the leeks and potatoes on the grill, cut side down. Cover and cook for 5 minutes, or until crisp grill marks appear.

7. Remove the leeks from the grill. Cool, then slice.

8. Flip the potatoes. Cover and cook for 5 minutes, or until crisp grill marks appear, then remove from the grill. Let cool, then chop.

9. In a large, oven-safe Dutch oven, heat the neutral oil over medium heat on the stove until the Dutch oven is slick and shiny.

10. Add the leeks, celery, and garlic to the Dutch oven with a dash of salt. Sauté 3 to 5 minutes, or until very fragrant.

11. Add the soybean paste to the Dutch oven, stirring to incorporate thoroughly, about 1 minute.

12. Add the chorizo, stew meat, potatoes, and kimchi. Sauté 2 to 3 minutes, stirring to coat all of the ingredients in soybean paste.

13. Add the chicken stock to the Dutch oven, stirring to incorporate.

14. Transfer the Dutch oven to the grill.

15. Lower the grill heat to 350°F and scatter the wood chips around the Dutch oven.

16. Cover and cook for 1½ to 2 hours, or until the stew meat is fork-tender. Check the stew every 15 minutes or so, adding more stock if necessary. You can continue reducing the stew to your desired consistency.

17. Remove the stew from the grill. Season to taste with salt, sugar, and lemon juice.

18. Garnish the stew with basil to serve.

PRO TIP

Don't throw away the leek tops! They are full of flavor and great sautéed on top of eggs, swirled into a silky soup, or even used to top this soup if you're a leek lover.

LEMONGRASS-MARINATED PORK LOINS WITH PICKLED CUCUMBERS AND CARROTS

The holy trinity of fish sauce, sugar, and lemongrass is what makes these pork loins so irresistible. The sugar caramelizes on the grill while the lemongrass releases its zesty fragrance and the fish sauce its salty, briny umami. This combination is integral to many Vietnamese grilled pork dishes and very worthy of becoming part of your regular marinade rotation. Bonus points for serving all of this over some vermicelli noodles and nuoc cham (Vietnamese dipping sauce).

YIELD: 2–3 servings | **PREP TIME:** 15 minutes, plus 24 hours to marinate | **COOK TIME:** 25 minutes

2 (1-inch-thick) pork loins, approximately 1¼ pounds total

2 tablespoons fish sauce

1 tablespoon white sugar

3 stalks lemongrass, peeled and minced

2 cloves garlic, grated

1 tablespoon neutral oil

wood chips of choice, as needed (optional)

1 lime, sliced in wedges, to serve

FOR THE PICKLED CUCUMBERS AND CARROTS

2 to 3 small Persian cucumbers, sliced thinly

1 small carrot, sliced thinly

2 tablespoons rice vinegar

1 teaspoon white sugar

2 teaspoons fish sauce

1. In a small bowl, combine the fish sauce with the sugar, lemongrass, garlic, and oil and stir until well mixed.

2. Pour the mixture over the pork loins in a food-safe container, cover, and marinate for 24 hours in the refrigerator, turning the pork loins every few hours to ensure thorough coverage.

3. Remove the pork loins from the marinade and brush off excess liquid. Bring to room temperature, roughly 15 minutes.

4. Preheat the grill to 450°F. Add the wood chips, if using.

5. Place the pork loins on the grill. Cover and cook for 5 to 8 minutes, or until crisp grill marks appear.

6. Flip the pork loins. Cover and cook for another 5 to 8 minutes, or until the pork reaches an internal temperature of 135°F.

7. Remove the pork from the grill and allow it to rest 5 minutes before slicing.

8. Combine the cucumbers, carrot, rice vinegar, white sugar, and fish sauce in a small bowl and marinate for 5 minutes before serving.

9. Serve the pork with the pickles and lime wedges.

BEEF-SHIITAKE BURGER

Reduction, not elimination, is my approach to red meat as the topic of climate change becomes ever more pressing in our daily lives. By simply stretching the ground beef in this burger with a mix of mushrooms, you can deepen the flavor of your burger *and* help out Mother Earth at the same time. Make sure you cook down the mushrooms until they have given up all their water; otherwise, they won't bind well to the beef and your burger will fall apart on the grill. These are softer burgers than the traditional all-beef variety, so use a flat spatula (like a fish spatula) to flip them, and there is no need to squish them on the grill as they are cooking.

YIELD: 4 servings, makes 4 burgers | **PREP TIME:** 15 minutes | **COOK TIME:** 17–23 minutes

4 ounces cremini mushrooms, stems removed

6 ounces shiitake mushrooms, stems removed

mesquite wood chips, as needed

2 teaspoons neutral oil

1 pound 80/20 ground beef

1 tablespoon kosher salt

½ teaspoon ground pepper

½ teaspoon smoked paprika

¼ teaspoon granulated garlic

¼ teaspoon onion powder

4 burger buns of choice

neutral oil, as needed

---

1. Place the cremini and shiitake mushrooms in a food processor and process them into very small pieces, but stop before they turn into a paste.

2. Heat the oil in a large nonstick skillet on the stovetop over medium heat until the skillet is slick and shiny.

3. Add the mushrooms with a dash of salt and reduce the heat to medium-low. Cook, stirring intermittently, until the mushrooms have given up all of their moisture and lightly browned, roughly 8 to 10 minutes.

4. Preheat the grill to 450°F. Place the wood chips onto the grill.

5. Remove the mushrooms from the skillet and place them in an even layer on a plate or sheet tray to cool.

6. Combine the beef with the cooled mushroom mix, salt, pepper, paprika, garlic, and onion powder in a large bowl. Work quickly with gloved hands to incorporate the mixture evenly, stopping quickly once the mixture is well combined.

7. Form the mixture into 4 equal patties.

8. Place the patties on the grill, cover, and cook for 3 to 5 minutes, or until crisp grill marks appear.

9. Flip the patties and cook, covered, for another 3 to 5 minutes or to desired level of doneness. For medium burgers, cook to an internal temperature of 140°F.

10. Remove the burgers from the grill and allow them to rest for 2 to 3 minutes.

11. Brush both sides of the burger buns with oil.

12. Place the burger buns on the grill, cut side down, cover, and toast for 2 minutes.

13. Flip the burger buns, cover, and toast for another 1 minute.

14. Remove the burger buns from the grill and assemble the burgers and buns, along with your desired toppings.

POMEGRANATE AND WALNUT HANGER STEAK

This recipe was inspired by Kebab-e Torsh, or Persian kebabs marinated in a pomegranate and walnut puree, that hails from the northern province of Gilan. The meaty flavors of the hanger steak counterbalance the tart pomegranate and herbaceous parsley. Pomegranate molasses, or the thick syrupy result of slowly cooking down pomegranate juice, is essential for the sweet-sour of the recipe; you can find pomegranate molasses at Middle Eastern grocery stores or online.

YIELD: 2–4 servings | **PREP TIME:** 15 minutes, plus 8 hours to marinate | **COOK TIME:** 10 minutes

1 pound hanger steak

2 teaspoons kosher salt

2 tablespoons neutral oil

¼ cup pomegranate molasses

⅓ cup shelled walnuts

2 tablespoons chopped fresh parsley

2 tablespoons chopped fresh cilantro

3 cloves garlic, chopped

kosher salt, to taste

1 lemon, sliced into wedges

FOR THE SLAW

½ cup pomegranate arils (seeds)

¼ cup celery, sliced thinly

¼ cup chopped parsley

2 cloves garlic, grated

2 tablespoons chopped red onion

2 tablespoons white balsamic vinegar

2 tablespoons extra-virgin olive oil

kosher salt, to taste

1. Sprinkle the salt over the hanger steak.

2. In a blender, combine the oil, pomegranate molasses, walnuts, parsley, cilantro, and garlic. Puree until smooth.

3. Rub the pomegranate and walnut puree over the steak.

4. Transfer the steak to an airtight container and marinate in the refrigerator for a minimum of 8 hours.

5. Preheat the grill to 500°F.

6. Remove the excess marinade from the steak by hand and bring the steak to room temperature, about 20 minutes.

7. Place the hanger steak on the grill. Cover and cook for 5 minutes, or until crisp grill marks appear.

8. Flip the hanger steak. Cover and cook for another 5 minutes, or until the internal temperature reaches the desired level of doneness. Hanger steak is best at medium rare or medium.

9. Take the steak off the grill and allow it to rest for 5 minutes.

10. Slice the steak and finish it with additional salt and lemon juice, if desired. Serve.

HARISSA-MARINATED FLANKEN RIBS

Harissa is a North African chili paste that will change your grilling game forever. You can buy prepared harissa at most grocery stores, or if you're looking for a good weekend activity, making some from scratch is a fun exercise that makes your home smell delicious. Harissa's combination of roasted chiles, tomato paste, and garlic with aromatic spices like caraway seeds, coriander, paprika, and cumin plus a drizzle of grassy olive oil works wonders to cut through fatty beef or lamb. I chose flanken-style short ribs as they grill up quickly and are easy to parcel out for a large group (pro tip: use kitchen shears, not a knife!), but you can also take harissa and short ribs in a different direction with a cast-iron pan over low heat and lots of wood smoke.

YIELD: 4 servings | **PREP TIME:** 10 minutes, plus 24 hours to marinate | **COOK TIME:** 15 minutes

wood chips of choice, as needed (optional)

2 pounds beef short ribs, flanken style

1 tablespoon neutral oil

1 tablespoon kosher salt

1 tablespoon soy sauce

½ cup harissa

1 tablespoon pureed chipotle peppers in adobo

1 tablespoon shrimp paste

juice of 2 lemons, to serve

1 scallion, minced, to serve

1. Combine the short ribs with the oil, salt, soy sauce, harissa, chipotle peppers, and shrimp paste in food-safe container. Mix thoroughly. Cover and let the mixture marinate 24 hours in the refrigerator.

2. Preheat the grill to 450°F. Add the wood chips, if using. Place the ribs on the grill. Cover and cook for 5 to 8 minutes, or until crisp grill marks appear.

3. Flip the short ribs. Cover and cook for another 3 to 5 minutes, or to your desired level of doneness.

4. Remove the ribs from the grill and top with the lemon juice and scallion.

5. Serve.

SHRIMP PASTE

Shrimp paste is an excellent condiment popular in Southeast Asian cooking. You can use either paste "cakes" that are sold in discs, or a jarred paste. Just keep in mind the former is usually saltier and the latter sometimes a little sweet and often packed in oil; always sample the paste before adding it to your sauce! Shrimp paste is readily available in international grocery stores or online.

CHAPTER 5

POULTRY AND DAIRY

YOGURT-MARINATED CHICKEN BREAST

Yogurt is a magical tenderizing tool—its lactic acid is milder than the citric acid often found in marinades, so it works more slowly. Because the bits of excess yogurt also cook on the grill, its sugars caramelize to form a crisp outside crust and provide a subtle tanginess throughout.

YIELD: 2 servings | **PREP TIME:** 10 minutes, plus 12 hours to marinate | **COOK TIME:** 10–13 minutes

2 boneless, skinless chicken breasts
(roughly 1.25 pounds combined)

kosher salt, to taste

1 cup plain whole milk yogurt

1 teaspoon ground turmeric

1 tablespoon garlic, grated

neutral oil, as needed

wood chips of choice, as needed (optional)

½ lime, sliced into wedges (optional)

FOR THE FENNEL AND CORIANDER SPICE RUB

3 tablespoons roasted pistachios

2 teaspoons toasted white sesame seeds

2 teaspoons whole black peppercorns

1 teaspoon fenugreek seeds

1 teaspoon black cumin

2 teaspoons whole coriander seeds

1 teaspoon whole fennel seeds

¼ teaspoon white sugar

1 teaspoon kosher salt

1. Place the chicken in a food-safe container and liberally sprinkle with salt.

2. In a small bowl, mix the yogurt, turmeric, and garlic. Slather the yogurt mixture on the chicken until it is thoroughly covered.

3. Wrap the chicken in plastic wrap and marinate in the refrigerator for a minimum of 12 hours.

4. Preheat the grill to 450°F. Add the wood chips, if using.

5. Remove the chicken from the refrigerator and remove excess yogurt by hand. Bring the chicken to room temperature, roughly 20 minutes.

6. Combine all of the ingredients for the spice rub in a spice grinder or blender, and pulverize into a fine powder.

7. Cover each chicken breast with 1 tablespoon of the spice rub.

8. Brush the chicken breasts with oil.

9. Place the chicken breasts on the grill, presentation side down. Cover and grill for 5 minutes.

10. Flip the chicken and reduce the heat to 400°F. Cover and grill for another 5 to 8 minutes, or until the internal temperature registers 160°F.

11. Remove the chicken from the grill and allow it to rest 5 minutes.

12. Sprinkle chicken with more spice rub and spritz with lime juice, if desired.

13. Slice chicken on the bias and serve.

LAPSANG-CURED DUCK BREAST

Duck may well be the most decadent of poultry options, so I like to counterbalance its fattiness and meatiness with a touch of smoky astringency from lapsang souchong, a black tea from China that is smoke-dried over pinewood to give it a distinctive aroma and richness other black teas simply cannot match. I use Pekin duck in this recipe as it is a little smaller, easier to handle, and typically less gamey than its counterparts Magret and Mulard. If you have an extremely fresh duck (such as one you're carving yourself), you may want to either "dry-age" it in your refrigerator (sprinkle salt all over and leave it uncovered on a resting rack) for a few days or soak it in milk overnight to draw out some of that iron flavor.

YIELD: 4 servings | **PREP TIME:** 15 minutes, plus 8 hours to marinate | **COOK TIME:** 25 minutes

4 Pekin duck breasts, scored

cherrywood chips, as needed (optional)

FOR THE BRINE

8 packets lapsang souchong tea (or equivalent in loose tea) (alternatively you can use English Breakfast, but it won't be as smoky)

¼ cup kosher salt

2 tablespoons white sugar

1 quart water

½ shallot, chopped

4 cloves garlic, chopped

FOR THE SCALLION-GINGER SAUCE

1 tablespoon minced garlic

2 tablespoons minced ginger

4 scallions, minced

2 teaspoons fish sauce

1 teaspoon soy sauce

¼ teaspoon white sugar

1 teaspoon rice vinegar

¼ cup neutral oil

1 teaspoon toasted sesame oil

---

1. Combine the lapsang souchong packets, salt, sugar, water, shallot, and garlic in a medium pot, and heat over low heat on the stove until all of the salt and sugar have dissolved. Cool to room temperature.

2. Add the duck breast to the brine and transfer to the refrigerator to marinate for 8 hours or overnight.

3. Remove the duck breast from the brine and pat dry with paper towels. Bring to room temperature, roughly 15 minutes.

4. Preheat the grill to 400°F. Place wood chips on the grill, if using.

5. To make the sauce, combine the garlic, ginger, scallions, fish sauce, soy sauce, sugar, and vinegar in a small bowl.

6. Heat the oils in a small pot on the stove over high heat for 3 to 5 minutes, or until the temperature registers somewhere between 275°F and 300°F.

7. Pour the hot oil over the garlic mixture and stir to combine. Marinate and cool at room temperature.

8. Place the duck breasts skin-side down in a large nonstick pan. Place the pan on the stove over medium-low heat. Render for 5 to 8 minutes, or until the duck skin has released the majority of its fat and is golden brown, leaving a thin, crispy golden brown crust.

9. Transfer the duck breasts to the upper rack of the grill. Cover and cook for another 5 to 8 minutes, or until the internal temperature registers 130°F.

10. Remove the duck breasts and allow them to rest for 5 minutes before slicing.

11. Serve with as much sauce as desired.

PRO TIP

Don't throw away that rendered duck fat! Strain it through a fine-mesh sieve and reserve in your refrigerator to use later. (It'll hold for up to 6 months!)

CHICKEN THIGHS WITH CHIPOTLE, ADOBO, AND ROSEMARY

Chipotle peppers in adobo sauce is a canned ingredient ubiquitous in most Latin grocery stores (and also available online) for good reason: it adds a tantalizing smoky, sour, and sweet flavor to everything it touches. You can use the two items separately—chipotles are ripe, smoked jalapeños, while adobo is made from tomato, garlic, and vinegar—but I like to puree them to form a versatile base that can be used for marinades (like this one) as well as soups and dressings. Rosemary and preserved lemon are a knockout pairing with this chipotle-adobo mixture, adding some top notes and green aroma when slathered on juicy chicken thighs. Remember that infrared grilling doesn't circulate as much hot, dry air as a regular gas or charcoal grill, so chicken skin will likely not behave the same way as you're used to; hence, I opt for boneless, skinless thighs.

YIELD: 3–4 servings | **PREP TIME:** 10 minutes, plus 1 hour to marinate | **COOK TIME:** 10 minutes

1 pound boneless, skinless chicken thighs (roughly 4 to 6 thighs)

kosher salt, as needed

1 tablespoon neutral oil

¼ cup pureed chipotle peppers in adobo

1 whole preserved lemon, seeds removed, minced

3 sprigs rosemary, leaves only, minced

4 cloves garlic, grated

wood chips of choice, as needed (optional)

1 lime, sliced into wedges (optional)

tomatillo salsa (optional)

1. Liberally sprinkle the chicken thighs with the kosher salt.

2. In a small bowl, mix together the oil, chipotle pepper puree, preserved lemon, rosemary, and garlic, and combine with the chicken thighs until they are evenly coated. Marinate for up to 8 hours.

3. Preheat the grill to 450°F. Add the wood chips, if using.

4. Place the chicken thighs on the grill, flat side (where skin side would've been) down. Cover and grill for 3 to 5 minutes, or until crisp grill marks appear.

5. Flip the chicken thighs, cover, and grill for another 3 to 5 minutes, or until the internal temperature registers 170°F.

6. Remove the chicken thighs from the grill and allow them to rest for 3 minutes before slicing.

7. Serve with lime, if desired, and a side of tomatillo salsa.

FIVE-SPICE BEER CAN CHICKEN

Cooking a chicken over an open beer can is a great way to introduce moist air into the cooking cycle and produces an ultra-juicy bird imbued with a lightly hoppy flavor that's also beautifully crisp on the outside. The choice of beer doesn't affect the ultimate taste of the chicken *too* much, so perhaps save your craft cans for drinking. I pair my beer can chicken with a five-spice seasoning for the warm undertone from the cinnamon and cloves and the licorice notes from the star anise—a perfect way to elevate chicken. Incorporate wood chips to add a smoky element.

YIELD: 2–4 servings | PREP TIME: 5 minutes | COOK TIME: 1 hour

1 (3- to 4-pound) whole chicken, innards removed

kosher salt, as needed

2 teaspoons white sugar

five-spice mix, to taste

neutral oil, as needed

1 (16-ounce) can beer of choice

mesquite wood chips or wood chips of choice, as needed

1. Preheat the grill to 450°F.

2. Thoroughly the dry insides and outside of chicken with paper towels, then salt both liberally.

3. Sprinkle sugar on the outside of the chicken.

4. Liberally rub insides and outside of chicken with five-spice mix.

5. Brush the oil over the outside of the chicken to coat.

6. Drink or pour out ¼ can of beer.

7. Prop the chicken on top of the can by sticking the can into the chicken cavity and forming a tripod base with its legs so the chicken can stand comfortably upright.

8. Place the chicken on the grill and surround it with wood chips.

9. Cover the grill and cook for 20 minutes.

10. Reduce the heat to 350°F and cook another 40 minutes, until the thickest part of the chicken thigh registers 170°F.

11. Remove the chicken from the grill and cool for 10 minutes before carving.

12. Carve and serve with bright vegetable sides, such as grilled corn, a mayonnaise-free potato salad, or pickles!

FIVE-SPICE SEASONING

Five-spice mix is a blend of cinnamon, star anise, fennel seed, Sichuan peppercorn, and clove that's fabulous for poultry and pork.

Don't be afraid of the giblets! Chicken hearts are a great source of protein, iron, riboflavin, and zinc. They are also extremely inexpensive and readily available at your local butcher or supermarket—usually you'll find them next to chicken livers (another excellent offal). They don't have a particularly strong taste, and their texture when cooked properly is somewhere between that of chicken breast and calamari. The sake in this recipe helps extract the slightly metallic twang from chicken hearts, while the grill helps round out the flavor.

YIELD: 4 servings | **PREP TIME:** 10 minutes, plus 8 hours to marinate | **COOK TIME:** 8–10 minutes

1 pound chicken hearts

¼ cup soy sauce

1 tablespoon maple syrup

2 tablespoons sake

2 teaspoons rice vinegar

2 teaspoons mirin

¼ teaspoon ground white pepper

1 tablespoon minced scallion

1 tablespoon minced garlic

1 tablespoon minced ginger

2 teaspoons neutral oil, plus more as needed

wood chips of choice, as needed (optional)

1 lemon, sliced into wedges (optional)

Jalapeño Soy Dipping Sauce
(page 115; optional)

1. Combine the chicken hearts with the soy sauce, maple syrup, sake, rice vinegar, mirin, white pepper, scallion, garlic, ginger, and oil in a suitably sized bowl. Marinate 8 hours or overnight in the refrigerator.

2. Remove the chicken hearts from the marinade and arrange on metal skewers. Bring to room temperature, roughly 20 minutes. Brush lightly with oil.

3. Preheat the grill to 450°F. Add the wood chips, if using.

4. Place the chicken heart skewers on the grill. Cover and cook for 5 minutes, or until crisp grill marks appear and the surface is lightly charred.

5. Flip the chicken hearts, cover, and cook for another 3 to 5 minutes, or until the internal temperature reaches 165°F.

6. Remove the chicken hearts from the grill and serve with lemon and Jalapeño Soy Dipping Sauce, if desired.

Consider yourself warned: these wings are addictive. As someone whose guilty pleasure is salt and vinegar chips, I knew something in this book *had* to involve vinegar powder. Yes, it is a specialty ingredient you'll likely need to order online, but once you do, you might find yourself turning everything into a "salt and vinegar" version! Because these wings are cooked using infrared radiation, the outside skin probably won't be as crisp as wings cooked over gas or charcoal, but the intense juiciness inside makes it well worth the trade-off. Feel free to adjust the amount of vinegar powder. Sometimes if I'm planning to eat a whole batch of these by myself, I'll add even more than listed.

YIELD: 2 servings | **PREP TIME:** 10 minutes | **COOK TIME:** 15–20 minutes

wood chips of choice, as needed (optional)

1 pound chicken wings

1 teaspoon kosher salt

¼ teaspoon ground white pepper

⅛ teaspoon granulated garlic

⅛ teaspoon onion powder

½ teaspoon white sugar

neutral oil, as needed

2 teaspoons white vinegar powder

¼ teaspoon white sugar

1 teaspoon kosher salt

¼ teaspoon smoked paprika (optional)

2 teaspoons minced scallion, to serve (optional)

1 tablespoon chili oil, to serve (optional)

1. Preheat the grill to 450°F. Add the wood chips, if using.

2. Pat the chicken wings dry with paper towels.

3. Toss the chicken wings in a large bowl with the salt, white pepper, garlic, onion powder, and sugar until well combined.

4. Brush the chicken wings with the oil on both sides.

5. Grill the chicken wings in batches to avoid overcrowding the grill. Place the wings skin-side down, cover, and cook for 10 minutes or until crisp grill marks appear.

6. Flip the chicken wings, cover, and grill for another 5 to 10 minutes or until internal temperature has reached 170°F.

7. In a small bowl, mix together the white vinegar powder, sugar, salt, and paprika, if desired.

8. Remove the chicken wings from the grill and toss them immediately with the white vinegar powder mix.

9. Top the chicken wings with scallion and chili oil, if desired.

I drew inspiration for this one-skillet meal from chana masala, a tomato-stewed garbanzo bean dish popular in India and Pakistan. I love garbanzo beans because they're filling, easy, and inexpensive; they're full of protein and nutrients; and they take on any flavor you desire. And don't throw away the bean water either! That murky liquid, called aquafaba, is a valuable ingredient in the kitchen, best known for emulating egg whites in baking preparations as well as yolks in vegan "mayonnaise." I also included fine strips of collard greens to incorporate all the goodness of collards without braising them for a long period of time. In fact, you might want to reach for collards the next time you're preparing a salad. They're truly delightful raw too!

YIELD: 2 servings | **PREP TIME:** 25 minutes | **COOK TIME:** 40 minutes

wood chips of choice, as needed

2 tablespoon neutral oil, divided

½ large yellow onion, diced

4 cloves garlic, grated

2 teaspoons minced ginger

kosher salt, to taste

1 tablespoon tomato paste

½ teaspoon whole cumin seeds

½ teaspoon whole mustard seeds

½ teaspoon fenugreek seeds

½ teaspoon roasted split coriander seeds or whole coriander seeds, toasted

¼ teaspoon whole black peppercorns

1 cinnamon stick

3 whole cloves

¼ teaspoon hing powder (optional)

¼ teaspoon turmeric powder

2 Roma tomatoes, diced

1 (14-ounce) can garbanzo beans, drained and rinsed

2 teaspoons fish sauce

2 cups unsalted chicken stock

4 large eggs

4 cups stemmed, thinly sliced collard greens

white balsamic vinegar or sherry vinegar, to taste

1. Preheat the grill to 400°F. Add the wood chips.

2. Grind the cumin, mustard, fenugreek, coriander, black peppercorns, cinnamon, and cloves in a spice grinder until coarsely ground. Transfer the seasoning blend to a small bowl and combine with the hing, if using, and turmeric powder.

3. Heat 1 tablespoon of oil in a medium, oven-safe cast-iron skillet on the stove over medium heat until the skillet is slick and shiny.

4. Add the onion, the garlic, the ginger, and a dash of salt. Reduce the heat to medium-low and sauté the mixture for 8 to 10 minutes, until the onions are lightly caramelized.

5. Add the tomato paste and cook for another 2 to 3 minutes.

6. Add another tablespoon of oil to the skillet and increase the heat to high.

7. Add the spices and cook for 1 minute.

8. Reduce the heat to medium and add the tomatoes and garbanzo beans. Sauté for another 2 to 3 minutes.

9. Add the fish sauce and chicken stock. Stir. Remove the skillet from the heat.

10. Place the skillet on the grill, cover, and cook for 10 minutes. The mixture should be bubbly and well reduced.

11. Reduce the heat to 350°F. Cook the mixture for another 5 minutes, or until there is roughly ½ cup liquid left in the skillet.

12. Carefully break the eggs on top of the mixture. Cover and cook for 2 minutes. Remove the cover and continue cooking the yolks to desired doneness.

13. Remove the skillet from the grill and top the mixture with collard greens. Stir to combine thoroughly.

14. Season to taste with salt and white balsamic vinegar.

ROASTED SPLIT CORIANDER SEEDS, HING POWDER, AND WHITE BALSAMIC VINEGAR

Roasted split coriander seeds are whole coriander seeds slowly roasted until they split in half. They are often used as breath fresheners in India, much like fennel seeds. Hing is a powder made from the dried resin of certain plants. It offers a unique, slightly oniony, deeply savory flavor that's most commonly associated with Indian cuisine. Roasted split coriander seeds and hing are available at Indian grocery stores or online.

White balsamic vinegar is quite different from the regular balsamic vinegar you may be used to. It's made from pressure-cooked white wine grapes (to avoid oxidation), then aged in barrels for a smooth, sweet yet tangy flavor that feels light on the tongue. It's a great choice for brighter salad dressings and, of course, juicy pickles.

Mussels in tomato broth layers many of the flavors we find pleasurable. Finishing the mussels on the grill with wood chips then also infuses them with a gorgeous smokiness. For me, it's reminiscent of gathering by a campsite to cook freshly caught clams after a long day in the water, the smells of pine trees and fire, and the darkness of a night sky without the distraction of city lights.

YIELD: 2 servings | **PREP TIME:** 25 minutes | **COOK TIME:** 60–65 minutes

1 tablespoon neutral oil

½ yellow onion, diced

6 cloves garlic, sliced

2 sausage links of choice, chopped

8 sprigs minced fresh oregano, leaves only

3 sprigs minced fresh rosemary, leaves only

2 bay leaves

8 sun-dried tomatoes, sliced

4 Roma tomatoes, chopped

2 tomatillos, halved and grilled, cut-side down, for 5 minutes, then chopped

½ teaspoon kosher salt

2 teaspoons soy sauce

1 teaspoon red pepper flakes

¼ teaspoon freshly ground pepper

1 cup dry white wine

1 pound live mussels, cleaned

1 tablespoon chopped fresh parsley, leaves only, to serve

1 tablespoon sliced fresh Italian basil, to serve

wood chips of choice, as needed (optional)

1. Heat the oil in large cast-iron skillet on the stove over medium until the skillet is slick and shiny.

2. Add the onion and garlic, along with a dash of salt. Cook until the onion is lightly caramelized, roughly 10 minutes.

3. Add the sausage, the oregano, the rosemary, the bay leaves, the sun-dried tomatoes, and another dash of salt. Continue to cook for 5 minutes.

4. Add the Roma tomatoes and tomatillos and cook for 15 minutes, or until half of the tomatoes' natural juices remain in the skillet.

5. Add the salt, soy sauce, red pepper flakes, and pepper. Stir to combine.

6. Add the white wine and remove the skillet from the heat.

7. Preheat the grill to 400°F. Add the wood chips, if using.

8. Transfer the cast-iron skillet to the grill, cover, and grill the tomato mixture for 20 minutes.

9. Pour the mussels on top of the tomato mixture, cover, and grill for another 10 to 15 minutes or until all the mussels have opened.

10. Remove the skillet from the heat, and top the mixture with parsley and basil.

GRILLED SWORDFISH WITH YUZU KOSHO

Yuzu kosho is a specialty fermented Japanese condiment made of chile peppers, yuzu peel (an aromatic citrus), and salt. It's tangy, a touch funky, salty, and just the right amount of assertive to add an interesting note to meatier fishes. (Yuzu kosho is readily available at Japanese groceries or online.) Purple shiso, also known as perilla, is a lovely herb that's part of the mint family but tastes much more herbaceous and warm (some liken it to a mix of basil and cinnamon). It provides an excellent lift to this dish, and will change the mind of anyone who feels ambivalent about fish. Purple shiso is available at most Korean and Japanese grocery stores and farmers markets; if it's not easy to find near you, you can substitute a mix of mint and basil.

YIELD: 2–4 servings | **PREP TIME:** 10 minutes | **COOK TIME:** 7–8 minutes

wood chips of choice, as needed (optional)

1 pound swordfish fillets, at room temperature

kosher salt, to taste

neutral oil, as needed

2 teaspoons yuzu kosho

½ teaspoon grated garlic

2 tablespoons minced purple shiso

½ lemon, juiced

1. Preheat the grill to 450°F. Add the wood chips, if using.

2. Salt and oil the swordfish fillets, then place them on the grill. Cover and cook for 5 minutes, or until crisp grill marks appear.

3. Flip the swordfish and cook, uncovered, for another 2 to 3 minutes or until their internal temperature reaches 140°F. Remove them from the grill and allow them to rest for 5 minutes.

4. In a small bowl, mix together the yuzu kosho, garlic, shiso, and lemon juice. Spread all of the mixture on top of the swordfish fillets to serve.

GRILLED WHOLE FISH WITH KALAMATA OLIVE RELISH

There's something about digging into a whole fish that just gives me the feels. Perhaps it's nostalgia—my mother would often pick out a live fish at the fishmonger, have it killed fresh, and cook it up for fish soup with loads of ginger and scallions for dinner. Perhaps it's being married to a man from the Florida coast and spending many a breezy afternoon eating fish at the pier together. I love serving this kalamata relish with fish because it is so flexible, suiting everything from bold sardine to mild John Dory and supple red snapper.

To avoid the age-old problem of fish sticking to the grill, ensure your fish is well dried, well oiled, and brought to room temperature prior to being placed on the grill. The grill should be well cleaned and very hot before the fish touches its surface. When flipping the fish, use a fish spatula or similarly wide metal spatula to flip the fish in one fell swoop to avoid breaking or tearing the skin.

YIELD: 2 servings | **PREP TIME:** 5 minutes | **COOK TIME:** 20 minutes

1 (2- to 3-pound) whole fish of choice, scaled, cleaned, and butterflied

wood chips of choice, as needed (optional)

kosher salt, to taste

½ shallot or ¼ small red onion, sliced thinly

¼ orange, sliced, halved

3 cloves garlic, sliced

6 to 8 sprigs fresh savory, thyme, or marjoram

neutral oil, as needed

FOR THE KALAMATA OLIVE RELISH

1½ tablespoons kalamata olives, chopped finely

2 tablespoons chopped fresh parsley, leaves only

1 tablespoon minced red onion

¼ cup high-quality olive oil

2 teaspoons sherry vinegar

½ teaspoon fish sauce

½ teaspoon ground pepper

white sugar, to taste

1. Bring the fish to room temperature for roughly 30 minutes before grilling. Dry inside and out with paper towels.

2. Preheat the grill to 450°F. Add the wood chips, if using.

3. Score the fish skin with 3 to 4 deep cuts, taking care to leave ¼ inch distance from spine.

4. Liberally salt the fish, both inside and out.

5. Stuff the fish's insides with layers of shallot, orange slices, garlic, and savory. Tie securely with 3 or 4 pieces of twine.

6. Brush the fish skin generously with oil.

7. Place the fish presentation-side down on the grill, cover, and cook for 5 minutes.

8. Reduce the heat to 400°F and continue to cook for an additional 5 to 8 minutes, or until crisp grill marks appear.

9. Carefully flip the fish and continue to cook for 8 to 10 minutes, or until juices run clear and the internal temperature reaches 130°F. Remove the fish from the grill and allow it to rest 5 minutes.

10. While the fish is cooking, combine all of the ingredients for the relish in a medium bowl and set it aside.

11. Serve the fish whole or filleted, with all of the relish.

PRO TIP

If you prefer a more pureed texture for the relish, blend everything and serve tapenade-style.

GRILLED ROCKFISH WITH PRESERVED LEMON BUTTER SAUCE

Rockfish is an excellent go-to fish for pairing, as it is lean, firm, and mild. Its flesh holds up better on the grill than a flakier variety like cod. I love this preserved lemon sauce as it's sour, sweet, and herbaceous, making you salivate and want more. The umeboshi paste, or Japanese sour plum paste, is optional but adds an interesting funkiness to the final topping; beyond this application, you can swirl it into all types of dressings, soups, and sauces for a hard-to-place fruitiness that will leave your guests wondering! (Umeboshi paste is available at Japanese grocery stores or online.)

YIELD: 2 servings | PREP TIME: 10 minutes | COOK TIME: 20 minutes

wood chips of choice, as needed (optional)

1 pound rockfish, skinless or skin-on, pin bones removed, split into 4 pieces

kosher salt, to taste

neutral oil, as needed

FOR THE PRESERVED LEMON BUTTER SAUCE

½ cup unsalted butter

2 tablespoons minced garlic

2 tablespoon minced shallot

2 teaspoons minced fresh marjoram

1 teaspoon umeboshi paste (optional)

1 teaspoon green peppercorns in brine, drained and minced

½ preserved lemon, chopped

1 teaspoon fish sauce

½ teaspoon white sugar, plus more to taste

¼ cup chopped fresh parsley

½ lemon, juiced

kosher salt, to taste

1. Preheat the grill to 450°F. Add the wood chips, if using.

2. Melt the butter in a medium skillet on the stove over medium heat.

3. Add the garlic and shallot with a dash of salt. Cook, stirring frequently, for 5 minutes or until the garlic is deeply fragrant.

4. Add the marjoram and cook for 1 minute

5. Add the umeboshi paste, if desired, and mix until well combined.

6. Add the green peppercorns, preserved lemon, fish sauce, and white sugar. Cook for another 2 to 3 minutes, until the flavors have melded together.

7. Add the parsley and cook for another 1 to 2 minutes, until the parsley is cooked through.

8. Add the lemon juice and cook for another 1 minute.

9. Remove the sauce from the heat and season with salt and sugar to taste. Set aside.

10. Liberally salt and oil both sides of the fish fillets.

11. Place the fish on the grill, skin-side down. Cover and cook for 3 to 5 minutes, or until crisp grill marks appear.

12. Carefully flip the fish, cover, and cook for another 2 to 3 minutes, or until the internal temperature reaches 130°F. Remove the fish from the grill and allow it to rest for 3 minutes.

13. Serve the fish with 2 to 3 tablespoons of sauce.

GOCHUJANG-MARINATED SHRIMP SKEWERS

Gochujang is a spicy and sweet chili paste central to Korean cooking. It's a beautiful deep red color, sticky with glutinous rice and full of umami from fermented soybeans. I especially love using it as a marinade for grilled items to create a nice crust and char, and if you're looking to spice up some "same old, same old" recipes, just try substituting it in place of tomato paste! I also incorporate some kelp in this recipe to double down on oceanic goodness; it's another common ingredient in Korean cooking, but is a little more difficult to find unless you live near a Korean grocery store like H Mart. I buy mine online at a specialty retailer named Burlap & Barrel, which sources theirs off the coast of Iceland. I know these ingredients may feel unfamiliar, which is why I've applied them to a staple like shrimp—I hope you'll break out of your comfort zone and try out these new flavors!

YIELD: 2 servings | **PREP TIME:** 5 minutes, plus 30 minutes to marinate | **COOK TIME:** 5–10 minutes

1 tablespoon gochujang

2 tablespoons soy sauce

1 teaspoon minced garlic

1 teaspoon kelp powder

1 tablespoon rice vinegar

½ pound medium shrimp

wood chips of choice, as needed (optional)

1 lime, juiced, to serve

2 scallions, sliced thinly, to serve

1. Combine the gochujang, soy, garlic, kelp, and rice vinegar in a small bowl. Mix thoroughly.

2. Add the shrimp and marinate for 30 minutes.

3. Preheat the grill to 450°F. Add the wood chips, if using.

4. Pierce the shrimp through metal skewers and place them on the grill. Cover and cook for 3 to 5 minutes, until lightly blackened.

5. Flip the shrimp and cook, uncovered, for another 1 to 2 minutes or until the shrimp is completely cooked through.

6. Remove the skewers from the grill. Carefully remove the shrimp from the skewers.

7. Serve the shrimp on a plate with a sprinkle of scallion and lime juice.

PRO TIP

There are many different sizes of shrimp, so if you are using larger or smaller shrimp make sure to adjust cooking times.

If you're used to feasting on scallops with cream and butter, allow this recipe to change your mind. This combination of garlic, sumac, ginger, and tomato is refreshing and light, bringing a ceviche-like quality to these plump sea scallops. I know the tomato water seems like a pain to make, but once you have some in stock you'll see how much it spruces up anything it touches. Don't throw away the pulp either—you can still make a great Grilled Tomato Sauce (page 106) with it!

YIELD: 2 servings | **PREP TIME**: 5 minutes | **COOK TIME**: 2–4 minutes

wood chips of choice, as needed (optional)

½ pound sea scallops (about 10 to 20)

1 tablespoon neutral oil

2 teaspoons minced garlic

2 teaspoons minced fresh thyme, leaves only

1 teaspoon sumac

½ teaspoon kosher salt

½ teaspoon grated ginger

2 Roma or similar-sized tomatoes, pureed

1. Preheat the grill to 450°F. Add the wood chips, if using.

2. Combine the scallops with the oil, the garlic, the thyme, the sumac, the salt, the ginger, and 1 tablespoon of the tomato puree.

3. Place the scallops on the grill. Cook, uncovered, for 1 to 2 minutes or until light grill marks appear.

4. Flip the scallops and cook for another 1 to 2 minutes, or to desired level of internal doneness.

5. Strain the tomato puree through a fine-mesh sieve or cheesecloth to catch its water.

6. Remove the scallops from the grill.

7. Dress the scallops with tomato water and additional salt, if desired.

SUMAC

Sumac is a bright-red berry that is dried, ground, and used to add a tart top note to many Middle Eastern dishes. It works as both a complement and a substitute for lemon, is nicely flaky for visual appeal and texture, and imparts a light, pink-red hue to liquids and broths. Sumac is available at spice retailers or online at specialty retailers like Burlap & Barrel.

GRILLED OYSTERS

Why shuck oysters when they will open naturally on the grill? This is one of my favorite oyster preparation methods because it (a) ensures you won't maul yourself with a shucking knife and (b) marries land and sea with the use of duck fat. By layering the umami found in oysters with that of rendered duck fat, these oysters absorb a complexity that I think goes beyond what you'll find in a plain ol' Rockefeller version. If you want to add a smoky touch, I recommend using alder for a subtly sweet and woody note that rounds out the citrusy touch of the pink peppercorn. Make sure to either balance your oysters carefully on the grill, or use a bed of salt in an oven-safe skillet to hold them in place; this way, you don't lose that delicious oyster juice as it cooks!

YIELD: 2 servings | **PREP TIME:** 5 minutes | **COOK TIME:** 15–20 minutes

wood chips of choice, as needed (optional)

1 dozen oysters of choice

¼ cup duck fat

1½ tablespoons ground pink peppercorns

1 clove garlic, grated

⅛ teaspoon white sugar

1 teaspoon chopped epazote (optional)

1. Preheat the grill to 400°F. Place wood chips on grill, if using.

2. Place the oysters directly on the grill grates, cup-side down, or arrange them securely in an oven-safe skillet (preferably cast iron) filled 1 inch with salt. Cover the grill and cook for 5 minutes, or until the oysters open at the seams.

3. Combine the duck fat, pink peppercorns, garlic, and sugar in a small skillet on the stove over low heat.

4. Cook for 2 to 3 minutes, or until the garlic is fragrant and golden brown, the sugar is dissolved, and the pink peppercorn is fragrant.

5. Remove the duck fat from the heat. Add epazote, if desired, and steep for 5 minutes.

6. Carefully remove the oysters from the grill and remove the top shell. Place the oysters back on the grill, on the grates or in the skillet.

7. Spoon about 1 teaspoon of duck fat mixture onto each oyster.

8. Cover and cook for another 3 to 5 minutes or until the oysters are very hot, potentially bubbling lightly at edges.

9. Remove the oysters from the grill. Let them cool for 5 minutes before serving, as the shells are very hot.

PINK PEPPERCORN AND EPAZOTE

Pink peppercorn is rarely sold ground, so I recommend buying some pink peppercorns whole and grinding them in a spice grinder. They are actually not related to black or white peppercorn, but rather are the berry of the Peruvian peppertree that is related to the cashew nut (thus making it unsuitable for those with nut allergies). They are beautifully pink, floral, and peppery in flavor but without the bite that's common in black peppercorn.

Epazote is an herb native to Central America, with long leaves that resemble a dandelion. It's used both fresh and dried, but the fresh variety is far more intense. It has a somewhat medicinal smell and taste uniquely its own that vaguely resembles oregano, mint, anise, and lemon all at once. It provides a great lift to ingredients like beans or corn (a classic pairing for the herb in Mexico), and I think it also pairs well with the salinity of oysters in this scenario for a very different herbal note. Epazote is available fresh at many Mexican or Central American markets, or online dried.

Is there a more classic combination than salmon with rosemary and lemon? I'd be amiss to leave it out of this grilling book, so here's my go-to base recipe for this family favorite.

YIELD: 2–4 servings | **PREP TIME:** 5 minutes, plus 2 hours to marinate | **COOK TIME:** 6–10 minutes

1 pound skinless or skin-on salmon fillets

2 sprigs rosemary, leaves only, minced

2 cloves garlic, grated

¼ teaspoon ground pepper

neutral oil, as needed

kosher salt, to taste

wood chips of choice, as needed (optional)

3 lemon slices

lemon wedges, to serve (optional)

1. Place the salmon in a glass bowl and toss with the rosemary, the garlic, the pepper, and enough oil to coat the salmon. Sprinkle with salt. Cover and let marinate for 2 hours in the refrigerator.

2. Preheat the grill to 450°F. Add the wood chips, if using.

3. Remove the salmon from the refrigerator and bring to room temperature, roughly 20 minutes.

4. Remove the bits of garlic and rosemary from the salmon.

5. Place the salmon fillets on the grill, skin-side down (if using skin on). Cook, uncovered, for 3 to 5 minutes or until crisp grill marks appear.

6. Place 3 slices of lemon on the grill, and place the rosemary sprigs on top of the lemon. Carefully flip the salmon on top of the lemon slices. Cook, uncovered, for 3 to 5 more minutes or to your desired level of doneness.

7. Remove the salmon from the grill and allow it to rest for 2 to 3 minutes.

8. Top the salmon with additional lemon wedges, if desired.

GRILLED LOBSTER WITH MISO BROWN BUTTER AND BLACKENED LEMON

A few years ago I spent some time in Portland, Maine, learning about the fish and shellfish distribution industry through a scholarship with the James Beard Foundation. It is a fascinating, difficult business: catches are often unpredictable; there's a very limited window of time during which products can be stored; and certain items must be imported, others bid on, and others purchased from one wholesaler to another. Lobster was a big part of the conversation up North. I heard many tales of lobster boats and lobster catchers, and also learned a very useful tip to tell how long a lobster has been in captivity: Lobsters attempt to fight when sequestered in too small of a space, so in lieu of using claws (which are bound), they bite off each other's antennae. The longer the lobster has been held in the tank, the shorter its antennae tend to be.

YIELD: 2 servings | PREP TIME: 10 minutes | COOK TIME: 15–20 minutes

wood chips of choice, as needed (optional)

1 (2½- to 3-pound) lobster, halved, claws and tail removed

kosher salt, to taste

neutral oil, as needed

2 lemons, halved

salt and freshly ground pepper (optional)

FOR THE MISO BROWN BUTTER

¼ cup unsalted butter

1 tablespoon sweet white miso

1. Preheat the grill to 450°F. Add the wood chips, if using.

2. Liberally salt the lobster and brush with oil. Grill the lobster in batches for 5 minutes each to avoid overcrowding the grill. Lower the heat to about 400°F, then make sure to cook the lobster thoroughly, or until the juices turn white and begin to coagulate. Lobster claws typically take 7 to 8 minutes per side and the split lobster tail and body about 5 minutes per side, with the grill covered and cut side down.

3. Add the lemons to the grill, cut side down, and grill for 5 minutes or until crisp grill marks appear.

4. While the lobster is cooking, melt the butter in a small saucepan on the stove over medium heat.

5. Once it is melted, continue to cook the butter until it is lightly brown, roughly 10 minutes. When the butter begins to foam, it is close to browning. Keep a careful eye on it, as it tends to burn very quickly.

6. Add the miso to the butter and stir to mix thoroughly.

7. Remove the miso butter from the heat and cool. Strain flavored butter into a small food-safe container. (You can save the caramelized miso to add to sauces and stews!)

8. Remove the lobster from the grill and allow it to rest for 5 minutes. Squeeze the lemon juice generously on top.

9. Serve the lobster with all of the brown butter, salt, and pepper, if desired.

PRO TIP

Don't throw away the lobster shells! Save them in the freezer with other scraps and make a delicious seafood stock!

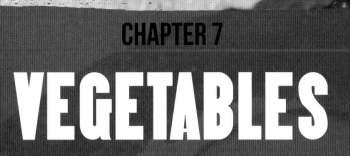

CHAPTER 7

VEGETABLES

Grilling avocados may feel a little odd, but do it once and you'll be sold. Make sure to choose barely ripe avocados to avoid a mushy mess on the grill, and move quickly to mix the avocado flesh with the lemon juice once they are finished grilling to stave off as much oxidation as possible. I've incorporated some za'atar here to intrigue avocado toast enthusiasts new and old; it's a condiment, dip, and spice mixture often used in the Middle East. While za'atar's exact combination varies from maker to maker, it typically includes thyme (the Arabic word za'atar means "thyme"), sumac, sesame seeds, and salt. Za'atar is readily available at most grocery stores, and online at specialty retailers like Burlap & Barrel.

YIELD: 2–4 servings, makes 4–6 toasts | **PREP TIME:** 5 minutes | **COOK TIME:** 5–8 minutes

wood chips of choice, as needed (optional)

2 barely ripe avocados, halved and pitted

neutral oil, as needed

kosher salt, to taste

2 tablespoons high-quality extra-virgin olive oil

1 tablespoon za'atar

1 lemon, juiced

kosher salt, to taste

4 slices bread of choice

1. Preheat the grill to 450°F. Add the wood chips, if using.

2. Brush the avocados with the neutral oil and sprinkle with salt.

3. Place the avocados on the grill, cut side down. Cook, uncovered, for 3 to 5 minutes or until crisp grill marks appear.

4. Flip the avocados and grill for another 1 minute. Remove the avocados from the grill and peel away the skin.

5. Mash the avocados and combine them with the olive oil, za'atar, lemon juice, and salt.

6. Place the bread on the grill. Cook, uncovered, for 2 to 3 minutes or until the bread is toasted to the desired level of crispness.

7. Remove the bread from the grill and slather with the avocado mash.

GRILLED ROMAINE VEGAN "CAESAR"

Grilled Caesar seems fancy, but really ought to be your next salad staple. It's warm and crunchy—two descriptors that I find many salads often cannot fill—plus it's very quick to grill up. This vegan "Caesar" is accessible for all potential guests without detracting from the unique umami Caesar dressing gives to the very juicy, but plain, vegetable that is romaine. The raw cashews provide a nice velvety mouthfeel while the nutritional yeast and miso give it depth and a certain mystery. You can make this dressing in larger batches and use it over the course of a week.

YIELD: 2 servings, makes ¾ cup dressing | **PREP TIME:** 20 minutes | **COOK TIME:** 5 minutes

wood chips of choice, as needed (optional)

2 heads romaine lettuce, halved (for smaller heads) or quartered (for larger heads)

kosher salt, to taste

FOR THE VEGAN "CAESAR" DRESSING

½ cup raw cashews, softened in 2 cups boiling water for 15 minutes or refrigerated in cold water for 8 hours, strained

1 teaspoon Dijon mustard

2 cloves garlic

¼ teaspoon white sugar

¼ teaspoon freshly ground pepper

neutral oil, as needed

15 cherry tomatoes, halved

2 teaspoons roasted sunflower seeds (optional)

1 teaspoon nutritional yeast

1 teaspoon sweet white miso

1 lemon, juiced

¼ cup neutral oil

¼ cup cold water

kosher salt, to taste

1. Preheat the grill to 450°F. Add the wood chips, if using.

2. Sprinkle the cut sides of romaine with salt and brush with oil.

3. Place the romaine on the grill, cut-side down, and cook for 5 minutes, uncovered, or until crisp grill marks appear and the outer leaves are charred.

4. Remove the romaine from the grill and place the cherry tomatoes on the grill, cut-side down. Cook, uncovered, for 1 to 2 minutes, or until blistered, then remove from the grill and set aside.

5. To make the dressing, combine the cashews with all of the other ingredients in a blender and blend until smooth. Season to taste.

6. Dress the romaine with 2 tablespoons of the "Caesar" dressing, adding more if desired, and top with tomatoes and sunflower seeds, if desired.

CORN OFF THE COB
WITH AVOCADO "GREEN GODDESS"

No street fair or summer gathering is complete without earfuls of corn poking out from patches of aluminum foil or skewered on a wooden stick. I absolutely love sweet yellow corn, but eating it on the cob is a rather messy affair so I've taken it off the cob and topped it with my favorite creamy dressing (fluffy and green from avocado!) as an alternative to a classic mayonnaise.

YIELD: 2–4 servings, makes ¾ cup dressing | **PREP TIME:** 15 minutes | **COOK TIME:** 30 minutes

wood chips of choice, as needed (optional)

4 ears of corn, husked

FOR THE AVOCADO "GREEN GODDESS"

½ Haas avocado, flesh only

1 tablespoon chopped fresh dill

1 tablespoon chopped fresh tarragon, leaves only

2 cloves garlic, sliced

½ shallot, chopped

½ jalapeño, seeded and chopped (optional)

1 tomatillo, husked, halved, and grilled

neutral oil, as needed

1 tablespoon chopped cilantro (optional)

¼ cup rice vinegar

½ cup neutral oil

¼ teaspoon freshly ground pepper

1 dash fish sauce (optional)

kosher salt, to taste

white sugar, to taste

1. Preheat the grill to 400°F. Add the wood chips, if using.

2. Brush the corn with the oil and place on the grill. Grill for 10 minutes.

3. Turn the corn sideways and cook for another 10 minutes. Flip the corn and cook for another 10 minutes, then remove it from the grill and let cool.

4. Combine all of the ingredients for the Avocado "Green Goddess" in a blender and puree until smooth.

5. Use a knife to take the corn off the cob on a cutting board. Stir in the Avocado "Green Goddess," 1 tablespoon at a time.

6. Top the corn with cilantro, if desired.

PRO TIP

Halve the tomatillos and grill, cut-side down, for 5 minutes or until crisp grill marks appear.

TRUMPET MUSHROOM "STEAKS" WITH SHIITAKE STEAK SAUCE

Before you turn up your nose at mushrooms masquerading as meat, give these plump trumpet mushrooms a chance! By crosshatching and grilling these mushrooms with hickory wood, you can capture much of the exterior texture of a classic steak *and* the scent of sizzling bacon. The natural heft of trumpet mushrooms is a surprisingly good imitation of meat (far better than the processed fake stuff, anyway). Pair this with a shiitake steak sauce to double down on that savory umami.

YIELD: 2–3 servings (makes 10 to 12 "steaks") 1 cup sauce | PREP TIME: 10 minutes | COOK TIME: 15 minutes

FOR THE MUSHROOM "STEAKS"

3 trumpet or king oyster mushrooms, sliced to about ¼ inch thick

kosher salt, to taste

neutral oil, as needed

hickory wood chips, as needed (optional)

FOR THE SHIITAKE STEAK SAUCE

1½ tablespoons neutral oil or unsalted butter	2 bay leaves
1 shallot, sliced	2 sprigs thyme
6 cloves garlic, sliced	¼ teaspoon ground black peppercorns
6 shiitake mushrooms, stemmed and sliced	¼ teaspoon ground white peppercorns
1 small carrot, peeled and chopped	1 teaspoon whole coriander seeds
1 teaspoon fish sauce	¼ teaspoon hing
1 tablespoon red or white miso	1 whole cinnamon stick
¼ cup dry white wine	kosher salt, to taste
1 quart unsalted chicken broth	lemon juice, to taste

1. In a medium rondeau, heat the neutral oil or butter for the steak sauce over medium heat until the rondeau is slick and shiny.

2. Add the shallot and garlic with a pinch of salt. Sauté for 3 to 5 minutes, or until the shallot is translucent.

3. Add the shiitakes and carrot with the fish sauce and sauté for another 3 to 5 minutes, or until the mushrooms have begun to shrink.

4. Add the miso and sauté for another 2 to 3 minutes, stirring to fully coat and lightly caramelize the vegetables.

5. Deglaze the pan with the wine and reduce the wine until the pan is nearly dry.

6. Add the chicken broth, bay leaves, thyme, black pepper, white pepper, coriander, hing, and cinnamon and bring to a light simmer.

7. Let simmer, uncovered, until the liquid has reduced to a quarter of the original amount (roughly 1 cup left), about 30 minutes.

8. Preheat the grill to 450°F. Add the hickory wood chips, if using.

9. Remove the sauce from the heat and let it steep for another 10 minutes.

10. Strain the sauce from the pan and season with salt and lemon juice to taste. If you prefer a super-thick steak sauce, you can also thicken this reduction with a cornstarch slurry.

11. Crosshatch one side of the mushrooms, then salt and oil them.

12. Place the mushrooms on the grill, crosshatched sides down. Cover and cook for 8 minutes, or until crisp grill marks appear and the entire side is golden brown.

13. Flip the mushrooms. Cover and cook for another 2 to 3 minutes, or until the mushrooms are fully cooked through.

14. Remove the mushrooms from the heat and serve with steak sauce.

GRILLED BUCATINI IN CREAMY MUSHROOM SAUCE WITH GRILLED MAITAKES

Yes, you can grill pasta! It's a delightful way to add some char to your noodle, not to mention a surefire method to avoid watery pasta-in-sauce. I chose bucatini, a plump cylindrical shape much like spaghetti but hollow inside. Because of its thickness, it is less likely to fall through the grill grates. You can also choose a regular spaghetti noodle, or even shapes like farfalle or bow ties—just stay away from super-thin and flat pastas like angel hair or linguine. The mushroom sauce is one of my favorites. Its creaminess comes from sunflower seeds and not cream, but you couldn't tell from its texture on the tongue! Paired with grilled maitake (which I usually like to grill alongside some pecan wood chips), ripe summer tomatoes, and tangy pecorino, this dish is a fair amount of work but *so* very worthwhile.

YIELD: 4 servings, makes 1½ cups sauce | **PREP TIME:** 20 minutes | **COOK TIME:** 45 minutes

wood chips of choice, as needed (optional)

2 (12-ounce) packages bucatini,
or pasta of choice

1 pound maitake mushrooms, trimmed
and portioned into segments

neutral oil, as needed

kosher salt, to taste

FOR THE CREAMY MUSHROOM SAUCE

2 tablespoons neutral oil

½ teaspoon hing powder

1 medium yellow onion, sliced

12 cloves garlic, sliced

1 pound cremini mushrooms, sliced

¼ cup chopped fresh oregano leaves

¼ cup dry white wine

1½ tablespoons soy sauce

25 cherry tomatoes, quartered

¼ cup chopped fresh parsley

¼ cup chopped fresh chives

¼ cup grated pecorino

1 lemon, in wedges

2 teaspoons fish sauce

2 teaspoons maple syrup

¼ teaspoon ground white pepper

⅓ cup roasted, unsalted sunflower seeds

2½ cups unsalted chicken stock

1 lemon, juiced

kosher salt, to taste

white sugar, to taste

1. Preheat the grill to 400°F. Add wood chips, if using.

2. To make the sauce, heat the oil in a large rondeau over medium heat on the stove until the rondeau is slick and shiny.

3. Add the hing powder and let sizzle for 30 seconds.

4. Add the onion and garlic with a dash of salt.

5. Lower the heat to medium-low and sauté until the onion is lightly caramelized, about 10 minutes.

6. Add the cremini mushrooms and oregano. Increase the heat to medium and sauté for 3 to 5 minutes, or until the mushrooms have reduced in size considerably.

7. Deglaze with white wine, and reduce the wine until the pan is nearly dry.

8. Add the soy sauce, fish sauce, maple syrup, white pepper, and sunflower seeds and sauté for another 1 to 2 minutes.

9. Add the chicken stock and bring the mixture to a light simmer. Let the mixture reduce for 5 minutes.

10. Remove the sauce from the heat and pour into a blender. Puree until very smooth, adding additional chicken stock if necessary.

11. Add the lemon juice, then season with salt and sugar to taste.

12. Transfer the sauce back to the rondeau.

13. Bring a large pot of water to a rolling boil on the stovetop. Add a large dash of salt.

14. Add the pasta and cook until just about al dente. Strain the pasta and toss liberally with neutral oil. *Do not discard the pasta water.*

15. While the pasta is cooking, brush the maitakes with oil and sprinkle them with salt. Place the maitakes on the grill, cut sides down. Cover and grill for 5 minutes, or until crisp grill marks appear.

16. Move the maitakes to the upper grill rack, cover, and let cook for another 5 to 8 minutes, or until fully cooked through.

17. Remove the maitakes and reserve.

18. Increase the grill heat to 450°F.

19. Heat the mushroom sauce in a large skillet over medium heat on the stovetop.

20. Place the pasta directly onto the grill in one even layer perpendicular to the grill racks. Let cook, uncovered, for 2 minutes, or until crisp grill marks appear.

21. Flip the pasta and let cook, uncovered, for another 2 minutes. Remove the pasta from the grill and immediately place it in the skillet with the mushroom sauce. Cook for another 2 to 3 minutes, until the pasta is well coated with sauce, adding additional pasta water if sauce begins to seize.

22. Place the pasta with the sauce onto four serving plates and top each with equal amounts of tomatoes, parsley, chives, pecorino, and lemon wedges.

PRO TIP

Hing, or asafoetida powder, is available at Indian grocery stores or online. If you don't have access to hing, you can simply remove it from the recipe.

GRILLED CABBAGE "COLESLAW"

It's no secret I love grilled cabbage (or any similar variation thereof, such as blackened cabbage, charred cabbage, and broiled cabbage). I've set off many a smoke detector in my apartment attempting to blacken cabbage for various salads, sides, and soups these last few years. This one of my favorite cabbage preparations—it makes a great substitute for traditional coleslaw as it brings a pop of color and flavor to the table. Try some for your next picnic!

YIELD: 4 servings | **PREP TIME:** 20 minutes | **COOK TIME:** 30–45 minutes

wood chips of choice, as needed (optional)

1 small head red cabbage, trimmed, cored, quartered

1 small head green cabbage, trimmed, cored, quartered

FOR THE DILL-TARRAGON DRESSING

½ cup neutral oil

1 teaspoon Dijon mustard

2 teaspoons honey of choice

¼ cup chopped fresh tarragon, leaves only

2 tablespoons chopped fresh dill

kosher salt, to taste

1 to 2 tablespoons neutral oil

1 teaspoon fish sauce (optional)

1½ tablespoons lemon juice

1 clove garlic, smashed

1 teaspoon fish sauce

kosher salt, to taste

freshly ground pepper, to taste

---

1. Preheat the grill to 450°F. Add the wood chips, if using.

2. Sprinkle the kosher salt on the cabbage and brush each cut side with the oil.

3. Place the cabbage on the grill, cover, and cook for 10 to 15 minutes, or until crisp grill marks appear and the entire side has browned.

4. Flip the cabbage to the second cut side, cover, and cook for 10 to 15 minutes, or until crisp grill marks appear and the entire side has browned.

5. Flip the cabbage to the rounded side, cover, and cook for 10 to 15 minutes, or until the cabbage is fully cooked through.

6. Remove the cabbage from the grill and let cool. Once cooled, slice thinly and toss with the fish sauce, if using.

7. Combine all the dressing ingredients in a blender and blend until smooth. Season with salt to taste, and toss with the cabbage to serve.

This recipe is an adaption of a delicious eggplant appetizer recipe I learned in Marrakech, Morocco, from Chef Edwina of House of Fusion last year. Her version uses baby eggplants charred on a gas stove; I've opted to grill them with pecan wood. Make sure you choose sweet smoked paprika, not just "paprika," as they are wildly different. Sweet smoked paprika is widely available in international grocery stores or online.

YIELD: 4–6 servings | **PREP TIME:** 10 minutes | **COOK TIME:** 45–60 minutes

pecan wood chips, as needed

4 Chinese or Japanese eggplants

1 tablespoon sweet smoked paprika

1 lemon, juiced

½ orange, juiced

2 tablespoons chopped fresh cilantro

2 tablespoons chopped fresh parsley

3 cloves garlic, grated

¼ cup high-quality extra-virgin olive oil

2 teaspoons white balsamic vinegar

¼ teaspoon ground white pepper

¼ teaspoon ground ginger

kosher salt, to taste

1. Preheat the grill to 450°F. Add the wood chips to the grill.

2. Place the eggplants, whole, directly on the grill. Cover and cook for 5 minutes, or until crisp grill marks appear.

3. Turn the eggplants. Cover and cook for another 5 minutes, or until crisp crosshatch marks appear.

4. Flip the eggplants. Cover and let grill for another 5 minutes, or until crisp grill marks appear.

5. Turn the eggplants again. Cover and let cook for another 5 minutes, or until crisp crosshatch marks appear.

6. Reduce the grill heat to 350°F. Place the eggplants on a rack or shelf inside the grill. Cover and cook for 20 to 30 minutes, or until the eggplants are completely soft at the center.

7. In a small bowl, mix together the paprika, lemon juice, orange juice, cilantro, parsley, garlic, olive oil, balsamic vinegar, white pepper, ground ginger, and salt.

8. Remove the eggplants from the grill and place them on a cutting board. Carefully slice off the stems and peel the eggplants. Leave whole if desired, or chop into smaller sections.

9. Cover the eggplants with the paprika mixture and serve.

The secret to these "pickles" is the white balsamic vinegar, which is quite different from the regular balsamic vinegar you may be used to. This vinegar is made from pressure-cooked white wine grapes (to avoid oxidation), then aged in barrels for a smooth, sweet, yet tangy flavor that feels light on the tongue. It's a great choice for brighter salad dressings and, of course, as a contrast to the light char on juicy pickles like this one. White balsamic is readily available at specialty grocers and online at Amazon.

YIELD: 4 servings, makes 1 quart pickles | **PREP TIME:** 10 minutes | **COOK TIME:** 5 minutes

wood chips of choice, as needed (optional)

6 small Persian cucumbers, halved

neutral oil, as needed

2 cloves garlic, grated

½ shallot, minced

1 teaspoon fish sauce

½ teaspoon white sugar

1 tablespoon white balsamic vinegar

1 tablespoon minced fresh dill

¼ teaspoon freshly ground pepper

kosher salt, to taste

1. Preheat the grill to 450°F. Add the wood chips, if using.

2. Toss the cucumbers with the salt and oil.

3. Place the cucumbers on the grill, cut side down. Cook, uncovered, for 5 minutes, or until crisp grill marks appear.

4. Remove the cucumbers from the grill and let cool.

5. Combine the cucumbers with the garlic, shallot, fish sauce, sugar, vinegar, dill, and pepper.

6. Mix thoroughly and season with salt to taste. Serve warm or cold.

This recipe combines a few of my favorite things across the world with a vegetable that's too often only served raw. Grilling snap peas gives them a substantial undertone that's well suited for this recipe.

Ponzu is a popular Japanese pantry item often used as a condiment or a marinade. It's soy based and roughly the consistency of soy sauce, but also contains various Japanese citrus such as yuzu and sudachi, in addition to mirin and dashi (stock from bonito fish and kombu seaweed). It's delightfully salty, sour, sweet, and aromatic and does a great job accentuating bright vegetables or lifting up heftier flavors.

Urfa pepper is a red Turkish pepper that's sun-dried, wrapped in plastic, and then ground with a touch of salt. It deepens to a stunning purple color and offers a smoky, salty, savory, sour note to everything it touches. Its flakes are also coarse, which adds interesting texture. Sumac is a bright-red berry that works as both a complement to and a substitute for lemon, is nicely flaky for visual appeal and texture, and imparts a lightly pink-red hue to liquids and broths.

YIELD: 4 servings | PREP TIME: 10 minutes | COOK TIME: 6 minutes

wood chips of choice, as needed (optional)

1 pound snap peas

1 tablespoon neutral oil

1 teaspoon kosher salt

2 tablespoons ponzu

1 teaspoon urfa pepper

1 teaspoon sumac

½ teaspoon smoked sweet paprika

1 lime, zested (optional)

1. Preheat the grill to 450°F. Add the wood chips, if using.

2. Toss the snap peas with the oil and salt.

3. Place the snap peas on the grill and cook, uncovered, for 5 minutes or until crisp grill marks appear.

4. Flip the snap peas, cover, and cook for another 1 minute or until they are bright green and fully cooked, but still crunchy.

5. Remove the snap peas from the grill and toss them with the ponzu, urfa, sumac, and sweet paprika in a large bowl. Top with lime zest, if desired.

At the beginning of my culinary career I spent some time in the R&D department of a French boulangerie. A large part of my work was creating, testing, and launching new tartines, or open-faced sandwiches, and naturally, radishes were a fan favorite given our French clientele. It may not be the most beloved vegetable in the States—yet! —but when paired with soft goat cheese and honey, I would argue radishes are a root vegetable like no other. The trick here is to make sure they're *just* barely cooked through, so each radish has absorbed the mesquite flavor but is still structured enough to be sliced thinly.

YIELD: 4 servings, makes 6 to 8 toasts | **PREP TIME:** 5 minutes | **COOK TIME:** 12 minutes

mesquite wood chips, as needed (optional)

10 radishes, stemmed

sliced bread of choice

soft goat cheese of choice, to taste

¼ cup chopped fresh parsley

honey of choice, to taste

kosher salt of choice, to taste

freshly ground pepper, to taste

1. Preheat the grill to 400°F. Add the wood chips, if using.

2. Place the radishes on the grill. Cover and cook for 5 minutes, or until crisp grill marks appear.

3. Flip the radishes, cover, and cook for another 5 minutes, or until crisp grill marks appear.

4. Remove the radishes and let cool. Slice thinly.

5. Place the bread on the grill. Cover and grill for 2 minutes, or until crisp grill marks appear.

6. Spread the goat cheese on the bread, top with the radishes, a sprinkle of parsley, a drizzle of honey, salt, and pepper.

GRILLED DELICATA SQUASH SALAD

Every year, the arrival of delicata squash is my mental demarcation between summer and fall. In my opinion, it's the very best squash and extremely underappreciated. The flesh is so sweet and creamy, the skin is edible (and tasty), it's easy to roast whole if desired and cut into rounds, *plus* the seeds are far simpler to remove than, say, butternut due to the delicata's shape. What's not to love?

YIELD: 2 servings | **PREP TIME:** 15 minutes | **COOK TIME:** 10 minutes

wood chips of choice, as needed (optional)

2 delicata squashes, halved lengthwise, seeded, and sliced into ½-inch-wide slices

kosher salt, to taste

neutral oil, as needed

FOR THE BALSAMIC VINAIGRETTE

2 cloves garlic

2 teaspoons chopped shallots

1 teaspoon chopped fresh oregano

1 teaspoon Dijon mustard

1 teaspoon maple syrup

4 ounces baby arugula

4 sweet mini bell peppers, sliced

¼ cup pomegranate arils (optional)

¼ cup goat cheese, crumbled

2 tablespoons high-quality balsamic vinegar

⅓ cup extra-virgin olive oil

kosher salt, to taste

freshly ground pepper, to taste

1. Preheat the grill to 450°F. Add the wood chips, if using.

2. Sprinkle the salt on the sliced delicata squashes and brush both sides with oil.

3. Place the delicata squashes on the grill, cover, and cook for 5 minutes or until crisp grill marks appear.

4. Flip the squashes, lower the heat to 400°F, and cook for another 5 minutes, or until the squashes are fully fork-tender. Remove from the grill.

5. In a blender, combine all of the ingredients for the balsamic vinaigrette and blend until smooth. Season with salt and pepper to taste.

6. In a suitably sized bowl, toss together the arugula, bell peppers, pomegranate, if desired, and vinaigrette. Place in a serving bowl.

7. Top the arugula mix with the delicata squashes and goat cheese.

Why boil potatoes for salad when you can grill them? This way, you can enjoy all the goodness of a potato crust, the scent of hickory wood, *and* the softness of the interior. I'm not a mayonnaise potato salad kind of person (why mask the tastiness of a good potato with all that mayo?) so this salad celebrates potatoes with lots of fresh herbs, good olive oil, and maybe a splash of sambal, or fresh chili paste, if you want to kick things into high gear.

YIELD: 2 servings | **PREP TIME:** 10 minutes | **COOK TIME:** 28–35 minutes

hickory wood chips, as needed (optional)

5 Yukon gold or red potatoes, skin on, halved

¼ cup apple cider vinegar

¼ cup ponzu

¼ cup extra-virgin olive oil

2 cloves garlic, grated

2 teaspoons sambal (optional)

¼ cup chopped fresh dill

¼ cup chopped fresh parsley

¼ cup chopped fresh sweet basil

2 stalks celery, sliced thinly

2 scallions, minced

kosher salt, to taste

white sugar, to taste

freshly ground pepper, to taste

1. Preheat the grill to 450°F. Add the wood chips, if using.

2. Place the potatoes on the grill, cut side down. Cover and grill for 8 to 10 minutes, or until crisp grill marks appear and the whole side is crispy.

3. Flip the potatoes. Cover and grill for 5 minutes, or until crisp grill marks appear.

4. Move the potatoes to the upper grill rack. Reduce heat to 350°F. Let cook for another 15 to 20 minutes, or until the potatoes are fork-tender and fully cooked through.

5. Remove the potatoes from the grill and let cool.

6. Chop the potatoes into bite-size pieces.

7. Combine the potatoes with apple cider vinegar, ponzu, olive oil, garlic, sambal if desired, dill, parsley, basil, celery, and scallions, and mix thoroughly to combine.

8. Season with salt, sugar, and pepper to taste.

If you've ever been the victim of soggy, brown broccoli, then let broccolini help you recover from that traumatic experience. It cooks significantly faster, allowing you to use just one cooking method to finish it properly, and it's sweeter and more tender to boot. I like to pair broccolini with oranges and sometimes almonds, as its lighter flavor works well with all types of dressings. But there's nothing wrong with just salt and pepper either!

YIELD: 2 servings | **PREP TIME:** 5 minutes | **COOK TIME:** 9–13 minutes

wood chips of choice, as needed (optional)

1 pound broccolini, stems trimmed

kosher salt, to taste

neutral oil, as needed

½ navel orange, sliced

2 teaspoons minced scallions (optional)

1. Preheat the grill to 450°F. Add the wood chips, if using.

2. Salt the broccolini and brush with oil.

3. Add the broccolini to the grill in one layer, cover, and grill for 4 to 5 minutes.

4. Flip the broccolini, reduce the heat to 400°F, and grill for another 3 to 5 minutes, or until the leaves are lightly charred and the insides are al dente. Remove from the grill.

5. Add the orange slices to the grill in one layer and grill for 2 to 3 minutes, or until crisp grill marks appear.

6. Squeeze the juice of the charred orange over the broccolini and top with scallions, if desired.

CHAPTER 8
SAUCES, MARINADES, AND MISCELLANEOUS

GRILLED TOMATO SAUCE

This tomato sauce is one of my signature sauces. I've made it for everyone, including friends, family, and a whole heck of a lot of clients. (It's also easily made into tomato soup with the addition of some potato and chicken broth or heavy cream!) Naturally, I figured it could benefit from some grilled tomato action, so here is a version with grilled tomatoes. Don't be startled by the addition of mushrooms—they are so well incorporated into the sauce, even mushroom haters won't notice or may even say the magical words, "There's something different here ... I like it." If you can, choose heirloom tomatoes at the height of the season; otherwise, regular beefsteak tomatoes will do.

YIELD: 1 quart | PREP TIME: 5 minutes | COOK TIME: 1½ hours

wood chips of choice, as needed (optional)

6 large tomatoes, halved

1 tablespoon neutral oil

1 medium yellow onion, sliced

8 cloves garlic, sliced

4 ounces baby bella mushrooms, sliced

1 teaspoon soy sauce

¼ cup dry white wine

2 sprigs fresh rosemary, leaves only

4 sprigs fresh thyme, leaves only

6 sprigs fresh marjoram, leaves only

2 fresh bay leaves

¼ cup tomato paste

1 teaspoon fish sauce

¼ teaspoon freshly ground pepper

10 whole allspice berries

½ teaspoon urfa pepper

¼ teaspoon whole cumin

1 quart unsalted chicken broth

kosher salt, to taste

sherry vinegar, to taste

---

1. Preheat the grill to 450°F. Add the wood chips, if using.

2. Place the tomatoes on the grill, cut side down. Cover and cook for 5 minutes, or until crisp grill marks appear.

3. Flip the tomatoes. Cover and cook for another 3 to 5 minutes, or until the tomatoes are cooked through.

4. Remove the tomatoes from the grill and let cool. Roughly chop and reserve.

5. In a large rondeau, heat the neutral oil over medium heat on the stovetop until the rondeau is slick and shiny.

6. Add the onion, the garlic, and a dash of salt. Cook, stirring intermittently, until the onion and garlic are both lightly caramelized, about 10 minutes.

7. Add the mushrooms and soy sauce and cook for 5 to 8 minutes, or until the mushrooms have given up most of their moisture.

8. Deglaze the pan with the white wine, and reduce the wine until the pan is nearly dry.

9. Add the grilled tomatoes, rosemary, thyme, marjoram, bay leaves, tomato paste, fish sauce, pepper, allspice, urfa, and cumin. Stir to combine.

10. Bring the mixture to a light simmer, and cook for 5 minutes.

11. Add the chicken broth and bring the entire mixture to a simmer. Turn the heat to low and simmer for roughly 45 minutes, or until the mixture has reduced by half.

12. Remove the bay leaves. Transfer the mixture to a blender and puree until very smooth.

13. Season with kosher salt and sherry vinegar to taste.

This basic vinaigrette utilizes any and all citrus you have available. The charred bits add a new element to something you're likely used to already, plus the addition of the pear lends body and sweetness while allowing you to use less oil and refined sugars.

YIELD: 1 cup | **PREP TIME:** 5 minutes | **COOK TIME:** 5 minutes

wood chips of choice, as needed (optional)	2 teaspoons Dijon mustard
2 oranges, halved	2 teaspoons minced garlic
1 grapefruit, halved	1 tablespoon minced shallot
1 lemon, halved	½ cup neutral oil
1 lime, halved	kosher salt, to taste
1 Bosc pear, peeled, cored, halved	¼ teaspoon ground white pepper

1. Preheat the grill to 450°F. Add the wood chips, if using.

2. Place the citrus and pear on the grill, cut side down. Cover and grill for 5 minutes, or until crisp grill marks appear.

3. Remove the citrus from the grill and juice. Transfer the juice to a blender.

4. Remove the pear from the grill and transfer to the blender.

5. Add the Dijon mustard, garlic, shallot, oil, salt, and white pepper to the blender. Puree until smooth.

6. Season with salt and white pepper to taste.

GRILLED PEACH AND GINGER DRESSING

Fruit in a salad, not so much. Fruit in a dressing, however, and you have my attention. This recipe highlights the best of summer peach season with a luscious dressing that pops with fresh ginger and cools with mint. I love it over bitter greens like kale or mustard, and it's also a surprisingly good substitute for ranch dip.

YIELD: 3 cups | **PREP TIME:** 5 minutes | **COOK TIME:** 15 minutes

wood chips of choice, as needed (optional)

2 ripe peaches, halved and cored

2 tablespoons minced ginger

4 cloves garlic

1 tablespoon chopped shallot

2 tablespoons chopped mint

2 lemons, juiced

1 lime, zested

½ lime, juiced

½ cup neutral oil

1 teaspoon fish sauce

¼ teaspoon freshly ground pepper

kosher salt, to taste

1. Preheat the grill to 450°F. Add the wood chips, if using.

2. Place the peaches on the grill, cut side down. Cover and grill for 5 minutes.

3. Turn the peaches. Cover and grill for 5 minutes.

4. Flip the peaches. Cover and grill for 5 minutes.

5. Remove the peaches from the grill and let cool.

6. Combine the peaches, ginger, garlic, shallot, mint, lemon juice, lime zest, lime juice, oil, fish sauce, and pepper in a blender and puree until smooth.

7. Season with salt to taste.

HABANERO HOT SAUCE

Using grilled shallots and tomatoes in this hot sauce gives an interesting underbelly to the floral top notes of habanero and bitter tartness of lime. If you're craving extra intensity, you can also char one of the habanero peppers or the carrot before adding them to the blender. This recipe also makes for an excellent canned sauce that can be given out as gifts or simply stockpiled in the cellar (who says the end of the world can't be filled with good eats, right?). Just make sure to check the pH levels of your final mixture to ensure it's suitable for boiling water canning, or else it will require pressure canning.

YIELD: 3 cups | PREP TIME: 5 minutes | COOK TIME: 25 minutes

wood chips of choice, as needed (optional)

2 shallots, halved

2 Roma tomatoes, quartered

1 tablespoon neutral oil

2 habanero peppers, seeded and chopped

½ cup chopped carrot

2 fresh bay leaves

6 cloves garlic

1 lime, juiced

1 teaspoon fish sauce

2 teaspoons shrimp paste

½ teaspoon toasted sesame oil (optional)

1 drop liquid smoke (optional)

kosher salt, to taste

white sugar, to taste

---

1. Preheat the grill to 450°F. Add the wood chips, if using.

2. Place the shallots and tomatoes on the grill, cut side down. Cover and grill for 5 minutes, or until distinct grill marks appear.

3. Flip the shallots and tomatoes. Grill, covered, for another 5 minutes or until crisp grill marks appear.

4. Remove the shallots from the grill and transfer to a blender.

5. Flip the tomatoes and grill, covered, for another 5 minutes or until crisp grill marks appear.

6. Transfer the tomatoes to the blender.

7. In a suitably sized skillet, heat the neutral oil on medium heat on the stovetop until the rondeau is slick and shiny.

8. Add the habanero peppers, carrot, and a dash of salt. Sauté for 5 to 8 minutes or until the peppers have softened and the carrots are fragrant.

9. Add the habanero peppers and carrot to the blender.

10. Add the bay leaves, garlic, lime juice, fish sauce, shrimp paste, sesame oil if desired, and liquid smoke if desired to the blender and puree until smooth.

11. Season to taste with salt and sugar.

12. Serve cold.

PRO TIP

Shrimp paste adds a fantastic nudge of umami to the sauce without overwhelming it. If you are allergic to shellfish, you can replace shrimp paste with fish sauce or yondu.

PRO TIP

Make sure to wear gloves while handling raw habanero peppers! For a completely smooth hot sauce, much like what you see in stores, add about ¼ teaspoon of xanthan gum to the mixture *while* the blender is moving at a low speed. Xanthan gum is a thickener and emulsifier, so it will smooth out the appearance of the sauce by swelling and binding to the water in the sauce.

Make this sauce once, and you'll find yourself dipping everything into it. The secret ingredient here is green Sichuan peppercorn oil, a zesty oil often used for its lightly numbing spiciness in regional Sichuan foods. It's available at Chinese grocery stores or online. However, if you don't have access to green Sichuan peppercorn oil, you can substitute toasted sesame oil for a slightly different—but still very delicious—outcome.

YIELD: 1 cup | **PREP TIME:** 5 minutes, plus 8 hours to marinate | **COOK TIME:** 5 minutes

wood chips of choice, as needed (optional)	**1 teaspoon maple syrup**
1 jalapeño, halved lengthwise	**¼ cup rice vinegar**
¼ yellow onion, sliced	**1 teaspoon green Sichuan peppercorn oil**
4 cloves garlic, sliced	**1 lime, zested**
½ cup soy sauce	**1 lime, juiced**
¼ cup water	**¼ teaspoon freshly ground pepper**

1. Preheat the grill to 450°F. Add the wood chips, if using.

2. Place ½ jalapeño on the grill, cover, and grill for 5 minutes or until crisp grill marks appear and the jalapeño is well softened.

3. Remove the jalapeño from the grill and slice, removing seeds if desired.

4. Combine the grilled jalapeño slices with the fresh jalapeño and all of the other ingredients in a covered food-safe container, and marinate for 8 hours or overnight.

This is the only recipe in the book that does not require the grill, but I promise you it's a worthy inclusion because of how great marinated items *taste* after being grilled! This marinade is loosely inspired by Jamaican jerk sauce, with its floral-sweet notes of allspice and heat from habanero peppers or Scotch bonnet; the latter is generally a little harder to find, but is well worth seeking out for its fruity and tropical notes. If you are worried about the heat, you can replace the peppers with habanada peppers, a new breed that has the taste of habanero with none of the hotness. This marinade is especially excellent for fatty cuts of poultry (like chicken or duck thighs!) and also as an accompaniment to meatier fishes like swordfish or grouper.

YIELD: 2 cups | **PREP TIME:** 10 minutes | **COOK TIME:** none

2 habanero or Scotch bonnet peppers, seeded, stemmed, and chopped

2 green bell peppers, seeded, stemmed, and chopped

3 cloves garlic

¼ teaspoon ground nutmeg

1 cinnamon stick

2 teaspoons whole allspice berries

3 tablespoons fresh thyme leaves

2 tablespoons chopped ginger

5 scallions, chopped

1 teaspoon kosher salt

2 teaspoons soy sauce

1 teaspoon fish sauce

¼ cup apple cider vinegar

1 tablespoon lime juice

2 tablespoons light-brown sugar

2 tablespoons canola or neutral oil

1. Combine all of the ingredients in a blender.

2. Puree until smooth.

3. Store in the refrigerator until use. Will last up to 1 month.

Hot or cold, this smoky onion jam is the perfect accoutrement for charcuterie spreads, burgers, sandwiches, and grilled meat platters. It's also my secret ingredient for soups and stews: I'll freeze a few dollops in ice cube trays so I can quickly use a few for a spontaneous hit of smoky, woody flavor.

YIELD: 2 cups | **PREP TIME:** 5 minutes | **COOK TIME:** 45–60 minutes

mesquite wood chips, as needed	**2 teaspoons maple syrup**
3 large onions, unpeeled, halved	**1 teaspoon fish sauce**
1 tablespoon neutral oil	**1 orange, juiced**
2 cloves garlic, grated	**1 cup unsalted chicken stock**
2 tablespoons balsamic vinegar	**kosher salt, to taste**

1. Preheat the grill to 375°F. Place the wood chips on the grill.

2. Place the onions on the grill, cut side down. Cover and grill for 15 minutes, or until well-charred grill marks appear.

3. Flip the onions and position them carefully so they are flat. Cover and grill for 1 hour, or until the onion juices are bubbling in between layers and the onions have cooked through completely.

4. Remove the onions from the grill. Carefully peel off the outer two layers that have blackened, then roughly chop.

5. Preheat the oil in a medium pot on the stovetop over medium heat until the pot is slick and shiny.

6. Add the onions with a dash of salt. Sauté for 5 to 8 minutes, or until the onions are lightly caramelized.

7. Add the garlic, balsamic vinegar, maple syrup, fish sauce, and orange juice, and sauté for another 2 to 3 minutes.

8. Add the chicken stock and reduce the heat to low.

9. Cook, uncovered, for 20 to 30 minutes, until all of the stock has evaporated and the mixture is thick, sticky, and chunky.

10. Transfer the onion mixture to a blender. Puree until smooth.

11. Serve hot or cold.

GRILLED CARROT AND APPLE SALSA

This carrot and apple salsa is my take on the Georgian (country, not state) dip of adjika, a well-loved spicy condiment made from a regional hot red pepper. It's popular in the Caucasus, with many different versions from various regions. I'll admit this combination of carrot, apple, onion, and red bell pepper sounded strange to me at first but after I ate just one spoonful I was completely sold. It's absolutely magical enjoyed with grilled meat, especially beefy cuts like hanger steak, or swirled into hummus, used as a crudité dip, or paired with charcuterie. It also holds up well canned, so why not make a big batch and store some for later? Just be sure to check the pH levels of your final mixture to ensure it's suitable for boiling water canning; otherwise, it will require pressure canning.

YIELD: 2 quarts | **PREP TIME:** 10 minutes | **COOK TIME:** 40–60 minutes

wood chips of choice, as needed (optional)

neutral oil, as needed

2 medium carrots, halved

1 Fuji or Gala apple, peeled, cored, and halved

1 small yellow onion, peeled and halved

1 red bell pepper, stemmed, cored, and chopped

1 jalapeño, stemmed and chopped

2 Roma tomatoes, chopped

1 tablespoon neutral oil

1 teaspoon kosher salt

1 teaspoon fish sauce

1½ teaspoons whole coriander seeds, coarsely ground

1½ teaspoons fenugreek seeds, coarsely ground

1 cup unsalted chicken stock

6 cloves garlic, grated

kosher salt, to taste

1. Preheat the grill to 450°F. Add the wood chips, if using.

2. Lightly oil the carrots, apple, and onion.

3. Place the carrots, apple, and onion on the grill, cut side down. Cover and grill for 5 minutes, or until crisp grill marks appear.

4. Transfer the carrots, apple, and onion to a food processor and process until evenly shredded in small chunks. Transfer to a suitably sized pot.

5. Place the bell pepper, jalapeño, and Roma tomatoes into the food processor, and process until evenly shredded in small pieces and the tomato is pulverized. Transfer to the pot.

6. Add the oil, salt, and fish sauce to the pot and place on high heat on the stovetop, stirring every few minutes, until the mixture comes to a boil. Reduce the heat to low.

7. Add the coriander and fenugreek seeds to the pot, stirring to distribute evenly throughout the mixture.

8. Let the mixture simmer for roughly 30 to 45 minutes, or until the moisture from the tomatoes and bell peppers has all but evaporated and the mixture is somewhat paste-like, but not burned on the bottom.

9. Add the chicken stock and garlic, mixing thoroughly. Bring the mixture back to a full boil and cook for another 5 to 10 minutes, or until the consistency is again thick and paste-like.

10. Remove from the heat and season with salt to taste.

11. Serve cold.

FENUGREEK

Fenugreek is a seed with a distinctive maple syrup smell, lightly bitter and herbaceous taste, and pellet-like shape. It adds a special layer of herbaceous complexity when used in spice mixes, and can also be roasted or even fried at high temperatures to mellow its flavor. Fenugreek is widely available at most international and Indian grocery stores, or online.

CHAPTER 9
SIDES AND DESSERTS

I love this sorbet because it's endlessly customizable. Blood oranges give this guilt-free sorbet its particular pink hue, but you can also use regular navel oranges if you're having trouble sourcing specialty ones. I love to use fresh lavender for this dessert, but if there's none available you can also substitute the fresh stuff for 1 tablespoon of dried food-grade lavender (which is readily available online). If you're not a fan of corn syrup, you can double the regular sugar and omit it, but the final texture of your sorbet will be a bit more like granita. To counteract this, you can puree the mixture with the flesh of 1 Bosc pear to give it a creamy body with no fillers and only a slight taste of pear.

YIELD: 2 cups | **PREP TIME:** 5 minutes, 1 hour to infuse, 2 hours to cool | **COOK TIME:** 25 minutes

wood chips of choice, as needed (optional)	½ cup white sugar
10 blood oranges or navel oranges	¼ cup light corn syrup
2 lemons, halved	1 teaspoon kosher salt
1 cup water	3 sprigs fresh lavender, leaves only

1. Preheat the grill to 450°F. Add the wood chips, if using.

2. Place the whole oranges on the grill. Cover and grill for 5 minutes, or until the skin is charred on one side.

3. Turn the oranges. Cover and grill for another 3 to 5 minutes, or until the skin is charred. Repeat until the majority of each orange is charred. Remove from the grill and let cool.

4. Place the lemons on the grill, cut side down. Grill, uncovered, for 3 minutes or until crisp grill marks appear.

5. Juice the oranges and lemons into a suitably sized container, using a strainer to remove the pulp. You'll need about 1 cup of juice.

6. In a small pot, combine the water, sugar, corn syrup, and salt. Bring to a light simmer on the stovetop, and whisk until the sugar and salt have dissolved.

7. Add the lavender to the pot and remove from the heat. Infuse for 1 hour.

8. Strain out the lavender and combine the syrup with the orange and lemon juice. Cool in the refrigerator for 2 hours, or until the mixture reaches about 40°F.

9. Process the mixture in an ice cream or sorbet machine according to manufacturer's directions.

If the traditional eggy ice cream base seems intimidating but the new-age eggless variety with commercial emulsifiers seems icky, look no further than this ultra-easy banana-based ice cream for a reliable ice cream experience. Grilling the bananas caramelizes their sugars and offers a deeper sweetness to the base, and throwing vanilla wafers into the mix makes this combination irresistible to parents and children alike. If you're interested in a slightly more savory version, try adding some crushed pretzels to the ice cream machine; for something decadent, try chocolate chips!

YIELD: 2 quarts | **PREP TIME:** 5 minutes | **COOK TIME:** 10 minutes

wood chips of choice, as needed (optional)

6 large bananas, halved but not peeled

1 cup heavy cream

1½ cups whole milk

¾ cup white sugar

½ teaspoon kosher salt

20 vanilla wafer cookies, such as Nilla Wafers

1. Preheat the grill to 450°F. Add the wood chips, if using.

2. Place the bananas on the grill, cut side down. Cover and grill for 5 minutes, or until entire side is well browned.

3. Peel the bananas and transfer to a blender.

4. Add the cream, milk, sugar, and salt to the blender. Puree until very smooth.

5. Let the banana mixture cool in the refrigerator until it reaches 40°F.

6. Place the vanilla wafers on the grill, flat side down.

7. Grill, uncovered, for 1 to 2 minutes or until crisp grill marks appear.

8. Remove the vanilla wafers from the grill and crush by hand into large chunks.

9. Process the banana base in an ice cream maker according to manufacturer's instructions.

10. As the ice cream maker is running, sprinkle the vanilla wafers into the base.

If you aren't already using a weight scale for baking, I encourage you to start now. Yes, you have to buy a small scale that calculates in grams (usually under $20 on Amazon), but just think: You'll never need to level a cup of flour again, or dig out chunks of butter from a measuring cup. Your recipes will turn out accurately *every* time. To be honest with you, I don't even bother following pastry recipes that aren't measured in grams because they are fundamentally inaccurate, and baking is not like cooking where things can be adjusted as you go. This scone recipe is one I've adapted from King Arthur Flour's excellent (and well-measured) website. It's a fantastic basic scone formulation that you can change up to your heart's desire with nuts, seeds, fruits, extracts, and more. I've also made this dairy-free so any lactose-intolerant guests don't have to miss out!

YIELD: 8–10 scones and 1 cup jam | **PREP TIME:** 10 minutes | **COOK TIME:** 35–45 minutes

FOR THE SESAME SEED SCONES

160 grams all-purpose flour

50 grams white sugar

¼ teaspoon kosher salt

1½ teaspoons baking powder

60 grams coconut oil, solid

1½ tablespoons toasted white sesame seeds

1½ tablespoons toasted black sesame seeds

2 large eggs

½ cup nondairy milk of choice

2 tablespoons honey

FOR THE SMOKY BERRY JAM

3 cups berries of choice

½ cup white sugar

½ teaspoon kosher salt

pecan or applewood chips, as needed

1. Whisk the flour, sugar, salt, and baking powder in a large bowl.

2. Add the coconut oil to the flour mixture, and combine using either a food processor or a pastry blender until the mixture is crumbly. *The mixture does not need to be completely evenly mixed, just as long as no giant chunks remain.*

3. Add the white and black sesame seeds to the flour mixture and stir to combine.

4. In a separate bowl, whisk together the eggs, milk, and honey until combined.

5. Add the flour mixture to the egg mixture, and stir with a spatula until the dough holds together. The dough will still be lightly crumbly, but when pressed together it should hold its shape.

6. Transfer the dough to a half-sheet tray fitted with parchment paper. Press the dough together to combine, and shape into a round, flat, hockey disc shape roughly 2 inches tall.

7. Cut the dough into 6 to 8 evenly sized triangles, placing them an equal distance apart on the tray.

8. Chill the dough in the freezer for 10 minutes. *This helps relax the gluten, which results in a more tender finished scone.*

9. Preheat the oven to 450°F. Add the wood chips.

10. Bake the scones on the upper rack of the oven for 10 to 15 minutes, or until golden brown. Remove the scones from the oven and let them rest for 5 minutes.

11. Combine the berries, sugar, and salt in an oven-safe skillet or a small Dutch oven. Stir to combine.

12. Place the skillet or Dutch oven on the grill. Cover and cook for 10 minutes.

13. Reduce the heat to 350°F. Stir the berry jam, taking care to scrape the sides.

14. Cover and cook for another 15 to 20 minutes, or until the jam has reduced to your desired consistency.

15. Remove the jam from the grill. Puree or mash to your desired consistency.

16. Serve the scones with a small side of jam.

CHAPTER 10
BEVERAGES

GRILLED PINEAPPLE DAIQUIRI

My husband is a mixologist, so naturally he wanted to use the infrared grill for some experiments behind the bar. I won't inundate you with all the wild things he made (homemade amaros with grilled peels, tinctures and syrups with charred wood chips, etc.), but I will say the grill brings a new layer of interest to alcohol infusions. This grilled pineapple rum plays into rum's dark, malty sweetness and lends it a maple-esque flavor that regular (nongrilled) pineapples can't. The result is of course great for a daiquiri, but you should also try it in some more unusual combinations like a Dark 'n' Stormy!

YIELD: 14 cocktails, makes 1 liter infused rum | **PREP TIME:** 5 minutes, plus 2 weeks to infuse | **COOK TIME:** 20 minutes

---

FOR THE INFUSED RUM

wood chips of choice, as needed (optional)

1 pineapple, peeled, cored, and cut into strips

1 liter rum (or other spirit of choice)

TO ASSEMBLE THE COCKTAILS

2 ounces infused rum, from above

1 ounce fresh-squeezed lime juice

¾ ounce demerara syrup

---

1. Preheat the grill to 450°F. Add the wood chips, if using.

2. Place the pineapple spears and core on the grill, cover, and grill for 10 minutes, or until crisp grill marks appear and the whole side is browned.

3. Flip the pineapple spears, cover, and grill for another 10 minutes, or until crisp grill marks appear and the whole side is browned.

4. Remove the pineapple spears from the grill and place in a nonreactive glass container. Pour rum or spirit of choice over pineapple spears to cover.

5. Wrap the container in plastic wrap and infuse at room temperature for a month. For a faster infusion, chop, then puree the grilled pineapple spears before combining with the liquor, then infuse for 2 weeks.

6. Strain the pineapple spears and charred bits from rum.

7. To make a cocktail, combine the infused rum, lime juice, and demerara syrup in a cocktail shaker with ice.

8. Shake vigorously, then strain and serve up in a coupe glass.

Sangria is a medium to which I like to apply anything I have in my refrigerator. Some extra fruit I had planned to use for pie? Sure. Leftover herbs or a spare fennel bulb from last night's roast chicken? Toss it in! The few tablespoons of jam, honey, or syrup at the bottom of a jar? Even better. Feel free to modify this recipe to your heart's liking so you can make the most of what's in season (Watermelon sangria? Apple sangria? Pomegranate sangria? Experiment as you wish!

YIELD: 4 servings, makes 1½ quarts | **PREP TIME:** 5 minutes, plus 4 hours to macerate | **COOK TIME:** 5–8 minutes

wood chips of choice, as needed (optional)

3 peaches, cored and halved

2 (750-milliliter) bottles white wine or rosé

¼ cup honey

1 pink grapefruit, sliced into triangles

1 navel or Cara Cara orange, sliced into triangles

10 sprigs mint, leaves only

5 (⅛-inch) slices ginger

2 sprigs sage, leaves only

1. Preheat the grill to 400°F. Add the wood chips, if using.

2. Place the peaches on the grill, cut side down, then cover and grill for 5 to 8 minutes.

3. Remove the peaches from the grill and let cool before slicing.

4. Combine the wine with the honey in a suitably sized container; stir until the honey has fully dissolved.

5. Add all of the other ingredients plus the peaches to the container with the wine. Cover and place in the refrigerator.

6. Let the sangria macerate for 4 hours before serving.

PRO TIP

A great choice of wine for white sangria is Vinho Verde, a barely effervescent low-ABV wine from Spain.

Take your standard Arnold Palmer (half lemonade, half tea) to the next level with genmaicha, a Japanese green tea that's combined with toasted brown rice for a rounded, nutty taste that suits the grilled lemons of this beverage exceptionally well. (It's readily available at Japanese grocery stores or online.) And speaking of lemons, if you're able to acquire some Meyer lemons, a hybrid variety crossbred with mandarins that's mellower in taste and sweeter on the nose, by all means use them here! For a special challenge, change out your regular honey here for something more assertive like maple-colored buckwheat honey with its woody and molasses undertones.

YIELD: 2 servings | **PREP TIME:** 5 minutes, plus 1 hour to cool | **COOK TIME:** 10 minutes

wood chips of choice, as needed (optional)

¼ cup genmaicha

2 cups 190°F hot water

2 tablespoons honey

4 or 5 Meyer lemons, halved

1. Preheat the grill to 450°F. Add the wood chips, if using.

2. Combine the genmaicha and hot water in a suitably sized food-safe container and steep for 3 to 4 minutes.

3. Strain out the genmaicha and stir in honey until fully dissolved.

4. Refrigerate genmaicha for 1 hour, or until cool.

5. Place the lemons on the grill, cut side down. Cover and cook for 10 minutes, or until well charred and softened.

6. Remove the lemons from the grill and juice to acquire about ¼ cup of lemon juice.

7. Stir together the chilled genmaicha with the lemon juice in the same container, and return the container to the refrigerator.

8. Once cooled, serve over ice.

PRO TIP

The ideal brewing temperature for tea is 190°F, not boiling (212°F) water.

Grilling the grapefruit and replacing some tequila with mescal amps up the smoky flavor of a classic Paloma. This version works especially well with hickory wood, but you can certainly try different varieties to find your favorite.

YIELD: 1 cocktail | **PREP TIME:** 10 minutes | **COOK TIME:** 20 minutes

hickory wood chips, as needed (optional)

2 large grapefruits, halved

½ ounce lime juice

½ ounce honey syrup

1 ounce mezcal

1 ounce tequila

ice cubes, as needed

3 ounces soda water (can be grapefruit flavored, if desired)

1 lime wheel

1. Preheat the grill to 450°F. Add the wood chips, if using.

2. Place the grapefruits on the grill, cut side down. Cover and grill for 10 minutes, or until crisp grill marks appear and the surface is well charred.

3. Flip the grapefruits, lower the heat to 400°F, and grill for another 10 minutes, or until the grapefruits are soft.

4. Remove the grapefruits from the grill and juice.

5. In a highball or collins glass, build the cocktail with grapefruit juice, lime juice, honey syrup, mezcal, and tequila.

6. Add ice cubes and top the cocktail with soda water.

7. Garnish with lime wheel.

HONEY SYRUP

Honey syrup is a derivative of simple syrup (1:1 ratio of sugar dissolved in water) that replaces sugar with honey at a ratio of 1.5:1 honey to water. Honey syrup can be made in batches and stored in the refrigerator for up to 2 weeks.

PRO TIP

For an extra-special treat, infuse your honey syrup with flavorings like lavender or thyme!

BACON-INFUSED OLD FASHIONED

Most people think of the Old Fashioned as an evening drink to be sipped by a fire with velvet shoes and maybe a cigar too—but it doesn't have to be! Bring this classic cocktail into the daytime using a technique called *fat washing*, essentially exploiting the liquid-to-solid properties of bacon to infuse both flavor and a smoother texture into a specific base alcohol. In a nutshell, when the bacon fat is still liquid, it's poured into the alcohol and shaken up, then frozen until it cools and beads at the surface before being skimmed off. Although the bacon fat is visibly gone, it can certainly still be tasted and felt in the final cocktail, making this Old Fashioned a perfect accompaniment for Sunday brunch or, honestly, anytime.

YIELD: 1 cocktail, makes 750 milliliters bourbon | **PREP TIME:** 5 minutes, plus 48 hours to infuse and another 4 hours to freeze | **COOK TIME:** 15–20 minutes

---

FOR THE BACON-INFUSED BOURBON
½ pound thick-cut bacon

750 milliliters bourbon of choice

FOR THE OLD FASHIONED
wood chips of choice, as needed (optional)

2 ounces bacon-infused bourbon

½ ounce simple syrup

3 dashes Angostura bitters

cocktail ice, as needed

1 flamed orange peel (see page 142 for how to make)

FOR THE BACON INFUSED BOURBON

1. Preheat the grill to 400°F. Add the wood chips to the grill, if using.

2. Place the bacon on a resting rack on a sheet tray, then place the tray onto the grill, working in batches so as not to overcrowd the rack.

3. Cover the grill and cook for 5 to 8 minutes, or until the bacon is crisp on top.

4. Flip the bacon, lower the grill heat to 350°F, and cover. Grill for 8 to 10 minutes or until well browned and crispy on all edges. You'll want to cook this bacon down a little further than strips you would eat in order to extract the most fat possible.

5. Repeat until all the bacon has been cooked. Remove the bacon from the grill, cool, and roughly chop.

6. Place the bacon bits in a suitably sized container. Cover with the bourbon.

7. Pour in all of the rendered bacon fat from the sheet tray. Cover the container and shake vigorously.

8. Wrap the container and infuse the bourbon in the refrigerator for 48 hours.

9. Place the bourbon in the freezer for 4 hours to solidify all drops of bacon fat.

FOR THE OLD FASHIONED

1. Add the bacon-infused bourbon, simple syrup, and Angostura bitters to a mixing glass with ice and stir for 30 seconds.

10. Strain the bourbon through a fine-mesh sieve, cover, and reserve in the refrigerator.

2. Strain into old fashioned or rocks glass with a large ice cube.

3. Garnish with flamed orange peel.

SIMPLE SYRUP AND FLAMED ORANGE PEEL

Simple syrup is merely white sugar dissolved in water in a 1:1 ratio.

A flamed orange peel sounds difficult but is actually a straightforward cocktail technique. Take one rectangular orange peel, leaving a slight shadow of the pith (so it's a little thicker than you might expect). Hold the peel in your nondominant hand with the skin facing the cocktail glass. Warm the peel slightly, using a lighter to heat the skin side of the peel for roughly 5 seconds, to help release the aromatic oils. Hold the lit lighter over the glass, and with the peel roughly 1 to 2 inches away from the flame, pinch the peel with your thumb and your forefinger—making sure to not drop the peel—to express the aromatic oils and let them spark into the flame. The charred oil will fall into the drink, and you can then rub the flamed peel along the sides of the glass for an extra hint of orange.

CONVERSION CHARTS

VOLUME

US	US Equivalent	Metric
1 tablespoon (3 teaspoons)	½ fluid ounce	15 milliliters
¼ cup	2 fluid ounces	60 milliliters
⅓ cup	3 fluid ounces	90 milliliters
½ cup	4 fluid ounces	120 milliliters
⅔ cup	5 fluid ounces	150 milliliters
¾ cup	6 fluid ounces	180 milliliters
1 cup	8 fluid ounces	240 milliliters
2 cups	16 fluid ounces	480 milliliters

WEIGHT

US	Metric
½ ounce	15 grams
1 ounce	30 grams
2 ounces	60 grams
¼ pound	115 grams
⅓ pound	150 grams
½ pound	225 grams
¾ pound	350 grams
1 pound	450 grams

TEMPERATURE

Fahrenheit (°F)	Celsius (°C)	Fahrenheit (°F)	Celsius (°C)
70°F	20°C	220°F	105°C
100°F	40°C	240°F	115°C
120°F	50°C	260°F	125°C
130°F	55°C	280°F	140°C
140°F	60°C	300°F	150°C
150°F	65°C	325°F	165°C
160°F	70°C	350°F	175°C
170°F	75°C	375°F	190°C
180°F	80°C	400°F	200°C
190°F	90°C	425°F	220°C
200°F	95°C	450°F	230°C

ABOUT THE AUTHOR

Jenny Dorsey is a professional chef, author, and artist specializing in interdisciplinary storytelling, fusing food with social good. She is the founder of Studio ATAO, a nonprofit immersive events studio, and runs her own culinary consulting business. She is the author of several books, including *Mastering the Instant Pot*, *Healthy Cocktails*, and *Air Frying for Everyone*, and her bylines have been published in outlets such as Eater, Michelin Guide, VICE, and Narratively. Her full biography, food portfolio, and written work can be seen at www.jennydorsey.co as well as her Instagram @chefjennydorsey. She lives in Los Angeles, California, with her husband and two dogs.